Kwasi Sarkodie-Mensah, PhD
Editor

Managing the Twenty-First Century Reference Department: Challenges and Prospects

Managing the Twenty-First Century Reference Department: Challenges and Prospects has been co-published simultaneously as *The Reference Librarian*, Number 81 2003.

Pre-publication
REVIEWS,
COMMENTARIES,
EVALUATIONS . . .

"VERY TIMELY. . . . AN IMPOR-
TANT GUIDE for reference
managers. . . . Offers valuable advice
in such areas as training and professional development, collaborative
leadership and team-based management, and quality service. This book
should be at the side of all reference
managers as they prepare to effectively lead their departments into the
new millennium."

Jamie Dendy, MLS
Head
Research & Instruction Services
Snell Library
Northeastern University

The Haworth Information Press
An Imprint of The Haworth Press, Inc.

Managing the Twenty-First Century Reference Department: Challenges and Prospects

Managing the Twenty-First Century Reference Department: Challenges and Prospects has been co-published simultaneously as *The Reference Librarian*, Number 81 2003.

The Reference Librarian Monographic "Separates"

Below is a list of "separates," which in serials librarianship means a special issue simultaneously published as a special journal issue or double-issue *and* as a "separate" hardbound monograph. (This is a format which we also call a "DocuSerial.")

"Separates" are published because specialized libraries or professionals may wish to purchase a specific thematic issue by itself in a format which can be separately cataloged and shelved, as opposed to purchasing the journal on an on-going basis. Faculty members may also more easily consider a "separate" for classroom adoption.

"Separates" are carefully classified separately with the major book jobbers so that the journal tie-in can be noted on new book order slips to avoid duplicate purchasing.

You may wish to visit Haworth's Website at . . .

http://www.HaworthPress.com

. . . to search our online catalog for complete tables of contents of these separates and related publications.

You may also call 1-800-HAWORTH (outside US/Canada: 607-722-5857), or Fax 1-800-895-0582 (outside US/Canada: 607-771-0012), or e-mail at:

docdelivery@haworthpress.com

Managing the Twenty-First Century Reference Department: Challenges and Prospects, edited by Kwasi Sarkodie-Mensah, PhD (No. 81, 2003). *An up-to-date guide on managing and maintaining a reference department in the twenty-first century.*

Digital Reference Services, edited by Bill Katz, PhD (No. 79/80, 2002/2003). *A clear and concise book explaining developments in electronic technology for reference services and their implications for reference librarians.*

The Image and Role of the Librarian, edited by Wendi Arant, MLS, and Candace R. Benefiel, MA, MLIS (No. 78, 2002). *A unique and insightful examination of how librarians are perceived–and how they perceive themselves.*

Distance Learning: Information Access and Services for Virtual Users, edited by Hemalata Iyer, PhD (No. 77, 2002). *Addresses the challenge of providing Web-based library instructional materials in a time of ever-changing technologies.*

Helping the Difficult Library Patron: New Approaches to Examining and Resolving a Long-Standing and Ongoing Problem, edited by Kwasi Sarkodie-Mensah, PhD (No. 75/76, 2002). *"Finally! A book that fills in the information cracks not covered in library school about the ubiquitous problem patron. Required reading for public service librarians." (Cheryl LaGuardia, MLS, Head of Instructional Services for the Harvard College Library, Cambridge, Massachusetts)*

Evolution in Reference and Information Services: The Impact of the Internet, edited by Di Su, MLS (No. 74, 2001). *Helps you make the most of the changes brought to the profession by the Internet.*

Doing the Work of Reference: Practical Tips for Excelling as a Reference Librarian, edited by Celia Hales Mabry, PhD (No. 72 and 73, 2001). *"An excellent handbook for reference librarians who wish to move from novice to expert. Topical coverage is extensive and is presented by the best guides possible: practicing reference librarians." (Rebecca Watson-Boone, PhD, President, Center for the Study of Information Professionals, Inc.)*

New Technologies and Reference Services, edited by Bill Katz, PhD (No. 71, 2000). *This important book explores developing trends in publishing, information literacy in the reference environment, reference provision in adult basic and community education, searching sessions, outreach programs, locating moving image materials for multimedia development, and much more.*

Reference Services for the Adult Learner: Challenging Issues for the Traditional and Technological Era, edited by Kwasi Sarkodie-Mensah, PhD (No. 69/70, 2000). *Containing research from librarians and adult learners from the United States, Canada, and Australia, this comprehensive guide offers you strategies for teaching adult patrons that will enable them to properly use and easily locate all of the materials in your library.*

Library Outreach, Partnerships, and Distance Education: Reference Librarians at the Gateway, edited by Wendi Arant and Pixey Anne Mosley (No. 67/68, 1999). *Focuses on community outreach in libraries toward a broader public by extending services based on recent developments in information technology.*

From Past-Present to Future-Perfect: A Tribute to Charles A. Bunge and the Challenges of Contemporary Reference Service, edited by Chris D. Ferguson, PhD (No. 66, 1999). *Explore reprints of selected articles by Charles Bunge, bibliographies of his published work, and original articles that draw on Bunge's values and ideas in assessing the present and shaping the future of reference service.*

Reference Services and Media, edited by Martha Merrill, PhD (No. 65, 1999). *Gives you valuable information about various aspects of reference services and media, including changes, planning issues, and the use and impact of new technologies.*

Coming of Age in Reference Services: A Case History of the Washington State University Libraries, edited by Christy Zlatos, MSLS (No. 64, 1999). *A celebration of the perseverance, ingenuity, and talent of the librarians who have served, past and present, at the Holland Library reference desk.*

Document Delivery Services: Contrasting Views, edited by Robin Kinder, MLS (No. 63, 1999). *Reviews the planning and process of implementing document delivery in four university libraries–Miami University, University of Colorado at Denver, University of Montana at Missoula, and Purdue University Libraries.*

The Holocaust: Memories, Research, Reference, edited by Robert Hauptman, PhD, and Susan Hubbs Motin (No. 61/62, 1998). *"A wonderful resource for reference librarians, students, and teachers . . . on how to present this painful, historical event." (Ephraim Kaye, PhD, The International School for Holocaust Studies, Yad Vashem, Jerusalem)*

Electronic Resources: Use and User Behavior, edited by Hemalata Iyer, PhD (No. 60, 1998). *Covers electronic resources and their use in libraries, with emphasis on the Internet and the Geographic Information Systems (GIS).*

Philosophies of Reference Service, edited by Celia Hales Mabry (No. 59, 1997). *"Recommended reading for any manager responsible for managing reference services and hiring reference librarians in any type of library." (Charles R. Anderson, MLS, Associate Director for Public Services, King County Library System, Bellevue, Washington)*

Business Reference Services and Sources: How End Users and Librarians Work Together, edited by Katherine M. Shelfer (No. 58, 1997). *"This is an important collection of papers suitable for all business librarians. . . . Highly recommended!" (Lucy Heckman, MLS, MBA, Business and Economics Reference Librarian, St. John's University, Jamaica, New York)*

Reference Sources on the Internet: Off the Shelf and onto the Web, edited by Karen R. Diaz (No. 57, 1997). *Surf off the library shelves and onto the Internet and cut your research time in half!*

Reference Services for Archives and Manuscripts, edited by Laura B. Cohen (No. 56, 1997). *"Features stimulating and interesting essays on security in archives, ethics in the archival profession, and electronic records." ("The Year's Best Professional Reading" (1998), Library Journal)*

Career Planning and Job Searching in the Information Age, edited by Elizabeth A. Lorenzen, MLS (No. 55, 1996). *"Offers stimulating background for dealing with the issues of technology and service. . . . A reference tool to be looked at often." (The One-Person Library)*

The Roles of Reference Librarians: Today and Tomorrow, edited by Kathleen Low, MLS (No. 54, 1996). *"A great asset to all reference collections. . . . Presents important, valuable information for reference librarians as well as other library users." (Library Times International)*

Reference Services for the Unserved, edited by Fay Zipkowitz, MSLS, DA (No. 53, 1996). *"A useful tool in developing strategies to provide services to all patrons." (Science Books & Films)*

Library Instruction Revisited: Bibliographic Instruction Comes of Age, edited by Lyn Elizabeth M. Martin, MLS (No. 51/52, 1995). *"A powerful collection authored by respected practitioners who have stormed the bibliographic instruction (BI) trenches and, luckily for us, have recounted their successes and shortcomings." (The Journal of Academic Librarianship)*

Library Users and Reference Services, edited by Jo Bell Whitlatch, PhD (No. 49/50, 1995). *"Well-planned, balanced, and informative. . . . Both new and seasoned professionals will find material for service attitude formation and practical advice for the front lines of service." (Anna M. Donnelly, MS, MA, Associate Professor and Reference Librarian, St. John's University Library)*

Social Science Reference Services, edited by Pam Baxter, MLS (No. 48, 1995). *"Offers practical guidance to the reference librarian. . . . A valuable source of information about specific literatures within the social sciences and the skills and techniques needed to provide access to those literatures." (Nancy P. O'Brien, MLS, Head, Education and Social Science Library, and Professor of Library Administration, University of Illinois at Urbana-Champaign)*

Reference Services in the Humanities, edited by Judy Reynolds, MLS (No. 47, 1994). *"A well-chosen collection of situations and challenges encountered by reference librarians in the humanities." (College Research Library News)*

Racial and Ethnic Diversity in Academic Libraries: Multicultural Issues, edited by Deborah A. Curry, MLS, MA, Susan Griswold Blandy, MEd, and Lyn Elizabeth M. Martin, MLS (No. 45/46, 1994). *"The useful techniques and attractive strategies presented here will provide the incentive for fellow professionals in academic libraries around the country to go and do likewise in their own institutions." (David Cohen, Adjunct Professor of Library Science, School of Library and Information Science, Queens College; Director, EMIE (Ethnic Materials Information Exchange); Editor, EMIE Bulletin)*

School Library Reference Services in the 90s: Where We Are, Where We're Heading, edited by Carol Truett, PhD (No. 44, 1994). *"Unique and valuable to the the teacher-librarian as well as students of librarianship. . . . The overall work successfully interweaves the concept of the continuously changing role of the teacher-librarian." (Emergency Librarian)*

Reference Services Planning in the 90s, edited by Gail Z. Eckwright, MLS, and Lori M. Keenan, MLS (No. 43, 1994). *"This monograph is well-researched and definitive, encompassing reference service as practices by library and information scientists. . . . It should be required reading for all professional librarian trainees." (Feliciter)*

Librarians on the Internet: Impact on Reference Services, edited by Robin Kinder, MLS (No. 41/42, 1994). *"Succeeds in demonstrating that the Internet is becoming increasingly a challenging but practical and manageable tool in the reference librarian's ever-expanding armory." (Reference Reviews)*

Reference Service Expertise, edited by Bill Katz (No. 40, 1993). *This important volume presents a wealth of practical ideas for improving the art of reference librarianship.*

Modern Library Technology and Reference Services, edited by Samuel T. Huang, MLS, MS (No. 39, 1993). *"This book packs a surprising amount of information into a relatively few number of pages. . . . This book will answer many questions." (Science Books and Films)*

Assessment and Accountability in Reference Work, edited by Susan Griswold Blandy, Lyn M. Martin, and Mary L. Strife (No. 38, 1992). *"An important collection of well-written, real-world chapters addressing the central questions that surround performance and services in all libraries." (Library Times International)*

The Reference Librarian and Implications of Mediation, edited by M. Keith Ewing, MLS, and Robert Hauptman, MLS (No. 37, 1992). *"An excellent and thorough analysis of reference mediation. . . . Well worth reading by anyone involved in the delivery of reference services." (Fred Batt, MLS, Associate University Librarian for Public Services, California State University, Sacramento)*

Library Services for Career Planning, Job Searching and Employment Opportunities, edited by Byron Anderson, MA, MLS (No. 36, 1992). *"An interesting book which tells professional libraries how to set up career information centers. . . . Clearly valuable reading for anyone establishing a career library." (Career Opportunities News)*

In the Spirit of 1992: Access to Western European Libraries and Literature, edited by Mary M. Huston, PhD, and Maureen Pastine, MLS (No. 35, 1992). *"A valuable and practical [collection] which every subject specialist in the field would do well to consult." (Western European Specialists Section Newsletter)*

Access Services: The Convergence of Reference and Technical Services, edited by Gillian M. McCombs, ALA (No. 34, 1992). *"Deserves a wide readership among both technical and public services librarians. . . . Highly recommended for any librarian interested in how reference and technical services roles may be combined." (Library Resources & Technical Services)*

Opportunities for Reference Services: The Bright Side of Reference Services in the 1990s, edited by Bill Katz (No. 33, 1991). *"A well-deserved look at the brighter side of reference services. . . . Should be read by reference librarians and their administrators in all types of libraries." (Library Times International)*

Government Documents and Reference Services, edited by Robin Kinder, MLS (No. 32, 1991). *Discusses access possibilities and policies with regard to government information, covering such important topics as new and impending legislation, information on most frequently used and requested sources, and grant writing.*

The Reference Library User: Problems and Solutions, edited by Bill Katz (No. 31, 1991). *"Valuable information and tangible suggestions that will help us as a profession look critically at our users and decide how they are best served." (Information Technology and Libraries)*

Continuing Education of Reference Librarians, edited by Bill Katz (No. 30/31, 1990). *"Has something for everyone interested in this field. . . . Library trainers and library school teachers may well find stimulus in some of the programs outlined here." (Library Association Record)*

Weeding and Maintenance of Reference Collections, edited by Sydney J. Pierce, PhD, MLS (No. 29, 1990). *"This volume may spur you on to planned activity before lack of space dictates 'ad hoc' solutions." (New Library World)*

Serials and Reference Services, edited by Robin Kinder, MLS, and Bill Katz (No. 27/28, 1990). *"The concerns and problems discussed are those of serials and reference librarians everywhere. . . . The writing is of a high standard and the book is useful and entertaining. . . . This book can be recommended." (Library Association Record)*

Rothstein on Reference: . . . with some help from friends, edited by Bill Katz and Charles Bunge, PhD, MLS (No. 25/26, 1990). *"An important and stimulating collection of essays on reference librarianship. . . . Highly recommended!" (Richard W. Grefrath, MA, MLS, Reference Librarian, University of Nevada Library)* Dedicated to the work of Sam Rothstein, one of the world's most respected teachers of reference librarians, this special volume features his writings as well as articles written about him and his teachings by other professionals in the field.

Integrating Library Use Skills Into the General Education Curriculum, edited by Maureen Pastine, MLS, and Bill Katz (No. 24, 1989). *"All contributions are written and presented to a high standard with excellent references at the end of each. . . . One of the best summaries I have seen on this topic." (Australian Library Review)*

Expert Systems in Reference Services, edited by Christine Roysdon, MLS, and Howard D. White, PhD, MLS (No. 23, 1989). *"The single most comprehensive work on the subject of expert systems in reference service." (Information Processing and Management)*

Information Brokers and Reference Services, edited by Bill Katz and Robin Kinder, MLS (No. 22, 1989). *"An excellent tool for reference librarians and indispensable for anyone seriously considering their own information-brokering service." (Booklist)*

Information and Referral in Reference Services, edited by Marcia Stucklen Middleton, MLS, and Bill Katz (No. 21, 1988). *Investigates a wide variety of situations and models which fall under the umbrella of information and referral.*

Reference Services and Public Policy, edited by Richard Irving, MLS, and Bill Katz (No. 20, 1988). *Looks at the relationship between public policy and information and reports ways in which libraries respond to the need for public policy information.*

Finance, Budget, and Management for Reference Services, edited by Ruth A. Fraley, MLS, MBA, and Bill Katz (No. 19, 1989). *"Interesting and relevant to the current state of financial needs in reference service. . . . A must for anyone new to or already working in the reference service area." (Riverina Library Review)*

Current Trends in Information: Research and Theory, edited by Bill Katz and Robin Kinder, MLS (No. 18, 1987). *"Practical direction to improve reference services and does so in a variety of ways ranging from humorous and clever metaphoric comparisons to systematic and practical methodological descriptions." (American Reference Books Annual)*

International Aspects of Reference and Information Services, edited by Bill Katz and Ruth A. Fraley, MLS, MBA (No. 17, 1987). *"An informative collection of essays written by eminent librarians, library school staff, and others concerned with the international aspects of information work." (Library Association Record)*

Reference Services Today: From Interview to Burnout, edited by Bill Katz and Ruth A. Fraley, MLS, MBA (No. 16, 1987). *Authorities present important advice to all reference librarians on the improvement of service and the enhancement of the public image of reference services.*

The Publishing and Review of Reference Sources, edited by Bill Katz and Robin Kinder, MLS (No. 15, 1987). *"A good review of current reference reviewing and publishing trends in the United States . . . will be of interest to intending reviewers, reference librarians, and students." (Australasian College Libraries)*

Personnel Issues in Reference Services, edited by Bill Katz and Ruth Fraley, MLS, MBA (No. 14, 1986). *"Chock-full of information that can be applied to most reference settings. Recommended for libraries with active reference departments." (RQ)*

Reference Services in Archives, edited by Lucille Whalen (No. 13, 1986). *"Valuable for the insights it provides on the reference process in archives and as a source of information on the different ways of carrying out that process." (Library and Information Science Annual)*

Conflicts in Reference Services, edited by Bill Katz and Ruth A. Fraley, MLS, MBA (No. 12, 1985). *This collection examines issues pertinent to the reference department.*

Evaluation of Reference Services, edited by Bill Katz and Ruth A. Fraley, MLS, MBA (No. 11, 1985). *"A much-needed overview of the present state of the art vis-à-vis reference service evaluation. . . . Excellent. . . . Will appeal to reference professionals and aspiring students." (RQ)*

Library Instruction and Reference Services, edited by Bill Katz and Ruth A. Fraley, MLS, MBA (No. 10, 1984). *"Well written, clear, and exciting to read. This is an important work recommended for all librarians, particularly those involved in, interested in, or considering bibliographic instruction. . . . A milestone in library literature." (RQ)*

Reference Services and Technical Services: Interactions in Library Practice, edited by Gordon Stevenson and Sally Stevenson (No. 9, 1984). *"New ideas and longstanding problems are handled with humor and sensitivity as practical suggestions and new perspectives are suggested by the authors." (Information Retrieval & Library Automation)*

Reference Services for Children and Young Adults, edited by Bill Katz and Ruth A. Fraley, MLS, MBA (No. 7/8, 1983). *"Offers a well-balanced approach to reference service for children and young adults." (RQ)*

Video to Online: Reference Services in the New Technology, edited by Bill Katz and Ruth A. Fraley, MLS, MBA (No. 5/6, 1983). *"A good reference manual to have on hand. . . . Well-written, concise, provide[s] a wealth of information." (Online)*

Monographic "Separates" list continued at the back

Managing the Twenty-First Century Reference Department: Challenges and Prospects

Kwasi Sarkodie-Mensah, PhD
Editor

Managing the Twenty-First Century Reference Department: Challenges and Prospects has been co-published simultaneously as *The Reference Librarian*, Number 81 2003.

The Haworth Information Press®
An Imprint of The Haworth Press, Inc.

New York • London • Victoria (AU)
www.HaworthPress.com

Published by

The Haworth Information Press®, 10 Alice Street, Binghamton, NY 13904-1580 USA

The Haworth Information Press® is an imprint of The Haworth Press, Inc., 10 Alice Street, Binghamton, NY 13904-1580 USA.

Managing the Twenty-First Century Reference Department: Challenges and Prospects has been co-published simultaneously as *The Reference Librarian*, Number 81 2003.

The development, preparation, and publication of this work has been undertaken with great care. However, the publisher, employees, editors, and agents of The Haworth Press and all imprints of The Haworth Press, Inc., including The Haworth Medical Press® and Pharmaceutical Products Press®, are not responsible for any errors contained herein or for consequences that may ensue from use of materials or information contained in this work. Opinions expressed by the author(s) are not necessarily those of The Haworth Press, Inc. With regard to case studies, identities and circumstances of individuals discussed herein have been changed to protect confidentiality. Any resemblance to actual persons, living or dead, is entirely coincidental.

Cover design by Lora Wiggins.

Library of Congress Cataloging-in-Publication Data

Managing the twenty-first century reference department : challenges and prospects / Kwasi Sarkodie-Mensah, editor.
     p. cm.
    "Co-published simultaneously as The reference librarian, number 81."
    Includes bibliographical references and index.
    ISBN 0-7890-2331-8 (alk. paper) – ISBN 0-7890-2332-6 (pbk. : alk. paper)
    1. Reference services (Libraries)–Management. 2. Academic libraries–Reference services–Management. 3. Library administrators. I. Sarkodie-Mensah, Kwasi. II. Reference librarian.
Z711 .M354 2003
025.5′2′068–dc22

                          2003022561

Indexing, Abstracting & Website/Internet Coverage

This section provides you with a list of major indexing & abstracting services. That is to say, each service began covering this periodical during the year noted in the right column. Most Websites which are listed below have indicated that they will either post, disseminate, compile, archive, cite or alert their own Website users with research-based content from this work. (This list is as current as the copyright date of this publication.)

Abstracting, Website/Indexing Coverage......... Year When Coverage Began

- *Academic Abstracts/CD-ROM* 1994
- *Academic Search: database of 2,000 selected academic serials,*
  updated monthly: EBSCO Publishing 1996
- *Academic Search Elite (EBSCO)* 1995
- *Academic Search Premier (EBSCO).* 1995
- *CNPIEC Reference Guide: Chinese National Directory*
  of Foreign Periodicals 1995
- *Current Cites [Digital Libraries] [Electronic Publishing]*
  [Multimedia & Hypermedia] [Networks & Networking]
  [General] <http://sunsite.berkeley.edu/CurrentCites/> 2000
- *Current Index to Journals in Education* 1992
- *Educational Administration Abstracts (EAA).* 1991
- *FRANCIS. INIST/CNRS <http://www.inist.fr>* 1983
- *Handbook of Latin American Studies* 1999
- *IBZ International Bibliography of Periodical Literature*
  <http://www.saur.de>. 1994
- *Index Guide to College Journals (core list compiled by integrating*
  48 indexes frequently used to support undergraduate programs
  in small to medium sized libraries) 1999

(continued)

(continued)

- *Referativnyi Zhurnal (Abstracts Journal of the All-Russian Institute of Scientific and Technical Information–in Russian)*.......... 1993
- *Sage Public Administration Abstracts (SPAA)*......................... 1991
- *SwetsNet <http://www.swetsnet.com>*............................... 2001

  *Exact start date to come.

Special bibliographic notes related to special journal issues (separates) and indexing/abstracting:

- indexing/abstracting services in this list will also cover material in any "separate" that is co-published simultaneously with Haworth's special thematic journal issue or DocuSerial. Indexing/abstracting usually covers material at the article/chapter level.
- monographic co-editions are intended for either non-subscribers or libraries which intend to purchase a second copy for their circulating collections.
- monographic co-editions are reported to all jobbers/wholesalers/approval plans. The source journal is listed as the "series" to assist the prevention of duplicate purchasing in the same manner utilized for books-in-series.
- to facilitate user/access services all indexing/abstracting services are encouraged to utilize the co-indexing entry note indicated at the bottom of the first page of each article/chapter/contribution.
- this is intended to assist a library user of any reference tool (whether print, electronic, online, or CD-ROM) to locate the monographic version if the library has purchased this version but not a subscription to the source journal.
- individual articles/chapters in any Haworth publication are also available through the Haworth Document Delivery Service (HDDS).

Managing the Twenty-First Century Reference Department: Challenges and Prospects

CONTENTS

ABOUT THE EDITOR

Kwasi Sarkodie-Mensah, PhD, is Manager of Instructional Services at the O'Neill Library, Boston College. He is also an adjunct professor in the College of Advancing Studies, where he teaches one session of the required research methods and data course to adult students. Dr. Sarkodie-Mensah is the author of over two dozen articles, several book chapters, and some 100 book and video reviews, and has presented several workshops on the difficult library patron issue. He is the editor of *Reference Services for the Adult Learner: Challenging Issues for the Traditional and Technological Era* and *Helping the Difficult Library Patron: New Approaches to Examining and Resolving a Long-Standing and Ongoing Problem* (The Haworth Press, Inc.).

Introduction

Kwasi Sarkodie-Mensah

Without the least doubt, the 21st century will be one of the most unique periods in the history of libraries. The rapid technological transformation in our society continues to affect every facet of our lives and livelihood. The paperless campus seems to be almost upon us even in the midst of skepticism. The Internet and the World Wide Web have had a tremendous impact in education, business, healthcare, transportation and other arenas, even if some areas seem to be light years behind. Libraries are among the areas where the influence of technology can be seen and felt. Reference services will continue to be the most conspicuous and dynamic of services to the user. Whether it is in a public, school, special, or academic library, it is very clear that the new head of 21st century reference will be facing many challenges. But these are exciting times for the people who lead the most conspicuous unit in many library systems. What are the challenges facing the 21st century head of reference? What are the prospects that avail themselves to propel the reference department into a vibrant future, and to prepare the reference library staff to embrace change and the opportunities to ultimately provide the best of service to users?

Many authors have expressed their views on the challenges facing the head of reference. For example, Fritch and Mandernack outline the challenges that face reference librarians in the new information envi-

[Haworth co-indexing entry note]: "Introduction." Sarkodie-Mensah, Kwasi. Co-published simultaneously in *The Reference Librarian* (The Haworth Information Press, an imprint of The Haworth Press, Inc.) No. 81, 2003, pp. 1-3; and: *Managing the Twenty-First Century Reference Department: Challenges and Prospects* (ed: Kwasi Sarkodie-Mensah) The Haworth Information Press, an imprint of The Haworth Press, Inc., 2003, pp. 1-3. Single or multiple copies of this article are available for a fee from The Haworth Document Delivery Service [1-800-HAWORTH, 9:00 a.m. - 5:00 p.m. (EST). E-mail address: docdelivery@haworthpress. com].

10.1300/J120v39n81_01

ronment. The 21st century head of reference must provide the vision that will put the user in the center of Fritch and Mandernack's responses to the new environment: digital reference services, web portals/gateways, searchable frequently asked questions, online tutorials, roving reference, research advisory sessions, peer mentors, reference exchange programs, staff training and staff hiring.[1]

Janet Balas mentions several transformations taking place in libraries and what libraries are doing about this in terms of services and planning for library buildings of the future–librarians having to evaluate new media format and their usability by users, provision of e-mail through the virtual library, instant messaging, or videoconferencing, planning for library buildings of the future to answer the needs of future generations, digitization efforts by libraries of materials of all kinds, including hard to find materials.[2]

The 21st century head of reference should have a role to play in these transformations. Contributors to the present work take a critical look at the challenges and prospects of the 21st century reference department. Lynda Leahy, in her "Managing an Academic Reference Department," affirms that even though the 21st century head of reference will require many of the same characteristics that were needed in the 20th century, the 21st century head of reference, who must be both an exceptional manager and an exceptional librarian, needs strong management expertise to deal with shrinking budgets, soaring costs, the endless proliferation of expensive electronic resources, and high expectations from users at all levels. In the piece, "From Core Competencies to Desired Traits: Hiring a Head of Reference for the New Millennium," Philip C. Howze examines some of the qualifications or desired traits librarians who are interested in head of reference positions should have. He contends that in an era when the number of candidates for head of reference positions continues to decline, and the dizzying rate of demand for electronic resources and fast-paced service continues to increase, getting ready for these services requires a very strong sense of preparedness so that we are not taken by surprise. The reference department of the 21st century will still have to provide services to users so accustomed to the changes in technology and its concomitant fast delivery of service. Justina Osa believes that the need for a visionary leader capable of "leading" a staff that is ready and capable of delivering this kind of service is a must for the library of this century. She explains this in her article "Managing the 21st Century Reference Department: Competencies." The retirement of baby boomers and the temptation to embrace work in the private sector have implications for reference management positions. The methods of hiring and retaining heads of reference need to be changed if we want to sustain leadership in reference, a unit of the library that most consider to be the most functional. Howze, in his piece "Training the New Head of Reference: Focusing on the Supervising Relationship as Technique," contends that one way of doing this for heads of reference in particular, and for other new supervisors, is to move people from previous supervisory experience–as a job requirement–to a willingness to participate in a positive and substantial training regimen. In 1991, Joseph C. Rost published *Leadership for the 21st Century*. Kathryn M. Crowe argues that Rost's leadership model of focusing on the influence relationship among leaders and followers rather than on the traits of the leader or the functions of leadership has applications to the academic reference department. In her article, "Collaborative Leadership: A Model for Reference Services," Crowe explores the model and its relevance in providing better job satisfaction for library staff as well as improved services to library users. In "It Takes a Village to Manage a 21st Century Reference Department," Paula McMillen and Loretta Rielly take a look at the Oregon State University's Valley Library's new management model used to run the reference department, its functioning, potential hazards, and multiple advantages. "The 21st Century Reference Department: Working to Provide Quality Service to Users" by Patience L. Simmonds stresses that the reference department in the 21st century needs, more than ever, the total collaboration of efforts and the utilization of the knowledge and expertise of all on board the service boat, including many outside the library, to meet the needs of users. Focusing on academic libraries and their reference departments, Felix Unaeze, in "Leadership or Management: Expectations for Head of Reference Services in Academic Libraries," delves into the dynamics of leadership and management, the changing roles of the reference library staff and their leaders or department heads. He also asks the question whether the reference head should be a manager or a leader.

REFERENCES

John W. Fritch and Scott B. Mandernack, "The Emerging Reference Paradigm: A Vision of Reference Services in a Complex Information Environment." *Library Trends*, Vol. 50, No. 2, Fall 2001, pp. 300-304.

Balas, I. Janet. Will there be libraries to visit in our future? (Online Treasures). *Computers in Libraries* 22 (2002): 41+. *Expanded Academic ASAP*. Gale Group Databases. Boston College, MA. 20 Apr. 2003. <http://www.infotrac.galegroup.com>.

Managing
an Academic Reference Department

Lynda Leahy

SUMMARY. To be an effective academic head of reference in the 21st century will require many of the same characteristics and skills necessary in the 20th century. While the traditional ways of providing reference services are changing, the fundamental need to provide access to information remains, and effective utilization of staff and other resources is paramount. Balancing the increasing pressures from shrinking budgets, growing costs, proliferation of expensive electronic resources, and high expectations from faculty and students creates a greater need for strong management expertise. The head of reference must be both an exceptional manager and an exceptional librarian. *[Article copies available for a fee from The Haworth Document Delivery Service: 1-800-HAWORTH. E-mail address: <docdelivery@haworthpress.com> Website: <http://www. HaworthPress.com> © 2003 by The Haworth Press, Inc. All rights reserved.]*

KEYWORDS. Reference librarians, library reference, World Wide Web, college and university libraries, management, supervision

Lynda Leahy is Associate Librarian, Harvard College for Research and Instruction, Widener 192, Harvard University, Cambridge, MA 02138 (E-mail: lleahy@fas. harvard.edu).

The author thanks Cheryl LaGuardia, Head of Instructional Services for the Harvard College Library, for her editorial advice.

[Haworth co-indexing entry note]: "Managing an Academic Reference Department." Leahy, Lynda. Co-published simultaneously in *The Reference Librarian* (The Haworth Information Press, an imprint of The Haworth Press, Inc.) No. 81, 2003, pp. 5-15; and: *Managing the Twenty-First Century Reference Department: Challenges and Prospects* (ed: Kwasi Sarkodie-Mensah) The Haworth Information Press, an imprint of The Haworth Press, Inc., 2003, pp. 5-15. Single or multiple copies of this article are available for a fee from The Haworth Document Delivery Service [1-800-HAWORTH, 9:00 a.m. - 5:00 p.m. (EST). E-mail address: docdelivery@haworthpress.com].

10.1300/J120v39n81_02

Many of the challenges that reference heads face today will continue into the foreseeable future. Flexibility must drive our thinking; the quality and agility of our outreach and communication with students and faculty will determine our effectiveness; the ability to manage both staff and resources skillfully is more crucial than ever; and recognizing and developing staff appropriately are key for meeting the challenge to provide dynamic reference services.

Access to information is and will remain at the heart of reference services. How that access is achieved is constantly evolving, and to be effective, the head of reference must be ahead of the curve, must be able to anticipate and plan for change, and must bring along the rest of the department on what sometimes is "a journey of the imagination." In other words, the 21st century head of reference must be primarily a visionary manager. This does not involve selling out to corporate America or becoming a faceless bureaucrat–the great fear of many academics in general and librarians in particular. It does mean that marshalling all the tools, skills, and resources available to us and using them creatively will be critical to future success.

Understanding how organizations operate and how to interact effectively with others within the organization has always determined, to some extent, the success or failure of any library manager. Business and service organizations in both the profit and non-profit worlds are acutely aware that growing user/customer expectations are challenged by finite resources and that staff are being called upon to do more with less. In the current economy it is only prudent to assume that we will continue to face reduced resources combined with soaring technological advances, costs, and user expectations. Therefore the real challenge before us is not just to learn how to cope but rather how to thrive in these conditions. Keep the words "flexibility" and "agility" in the forefront of your mind throughout this discussion as they are probably the two more important attributes a good head of reference can possess.

BEFORE THE HIRE

The quality of reference service depends on the skills of the librarians providing it, and identifying those skills must begin *before* the initial interview. The applicant résumé and cover letter are a first glimpse into a candidate's mind and reflect the image that he or she presumably wants to project. All the caveats that have been used before will continue to be true: misspellings, extravagant statements, wordiness, the inability to express an idea well, and poor presentation all cast a pall over the reader. However, now many librarians have posted Web pages–both personal and professional–that are easily found with a quick search, and since these pages are on the Web, they are fair game. Often these pages reveal far more than the résumé and cover letter, things that the applicant perhaps may not have wished to share. A wonderful article by Cheryl LaGuardia and Ed Tallent[1] describes in detail how a librarian should *not* use the Web. However, from the perspective of the head of reference who will be winnowing through countless résumés, the article also provides invaluable tips on what kinds of red flags to look for. One of the main advantages of advance Web searches on candidates is that the practice can reveal considerable information at minimal cost. Finding creative ways to get more information about candidates at low cost is going to determine who ends up with the best candidates in the shortest period of time.

An important criterion for hiring supervisors to use in a search is not to duplicate what you already have and most emphatically not to duplicate yourself. Look for complementary skills and experience. Try to develop a diverse staff. Look for people who can do what you cannot. While this may make you feel uncomfortable and less in control, it will result in a much stronger staff, because a homogeneous department lacks versatility, breadth, and flexibility, and it will become stagnant. A diverse staff will challenge themselves and you, and if you are willing to allow this challenge, it will also give you the opportunity to demonstrate your confidence in your staff as well as show your administration that you have confidence in yourself. It takes a secure manager to appreciate and hire individuals with diverse personalities and skill sets.

ON THE LINE

Working with and developing your staff is a full-time job. Being a library manager is not unlike being a coach in the National Football League. Your team is composed of different specialists, each of whom requires special attention and coaching. New librarians (rookies) need close attention to identify strengths and interests, provide emotional support, and offer encouragement to test their wings. Middle-range librarians (established players) may need to be shaken out of their routines and convinced that the old way of doing things is not necessarily the best way. You need to help them to identify ways to uncover latent skills and develop new ones. Long-term professionals (veterans), particularly those who have been in the same position for many years, need new challenges. In order to keep this group on their toes, you will need to identify hidden, often neglected talents. You will need to teach them new approaches and encourage them to stretch themselves, to think beyond what they have always done, and to share their experience and knowledge with newer staff. Every NFL team has a series of coaches–for offence, defense, receivers, etc. If you can view your senior librarians as part of your coaching staff and engage them in actively working with newer librarians, everyone benefits, which is key to working through transitional times.

To continue with the NFL analogy, the head of reference needs to scout the competition to find out what other academic reference operations are doing. What kinds of new approaches, new staff configurations, or new services are they using, and will any of those be applicable to your situation? How have other libraries with similar configurations and challenges addressed the same or similar problems to those you are facing? What kinds of priorities have they identified as the most important, and what have they done about those lower on the list? How have they implemented outreach to students and faculty? What kinds of expectations have been created, and how well have they been addressed? Reading professional literature is important, but actually talking with your counterparts can be much more meaningful. And it is just common sense to borrow from others; a scholar's best work rests on the shoulders of others. If everyone tries to develop an entirely new reference paradigm, the actual work of the department will be lost in the shuffle of keeping up with meetings and organizational development. Take from others what you can, and adapt it to address your local needs and mores.

Just as a football coach faces each season with high hopes and expectations so, too, do academic librarians face the beginning of each fall semester with renewed energy and enthusiasm. Our students and faculty are our fans, and we want to make them happy by identifying their wants and needs and–to the best of our ability within the strictures of budget and policy–satisfying them. While it is not always possible to provide all they need, we have to understand their perspective and align their priorities with our own. And most importantly, we must communicate with them so that they understand what has been decided and why. If you decide that you cannot afford to acquire a particular resource, let the requester know why and provide some alternatives. If you cannot provide a certain service, let the community know why and what their options are.

As head of reference, you are the manager and the supervisor, not a friend. While this is not by any means a new concept, it bears repeating. If you are to be an effective manager, you must be able to be as dispassionate as possible in making decisions. Personal feelings–either positive or negative–about particular individuals should not bear on what you do. Your decisions as a manager must reflect fairness and equal treatment and a long-range view of what is good for the department and the institution. This, of course, does not mean that you are distant and unapproachable, because it is equally important for your staff to understand that you are there for them and that you care about their well-being and professional development. But you are the individual, as head of reference, who needs to develop and maintain a long-range vision of what reference service means at your institution.

This can be a difficult balancing act for supervisors, especially those who have been promoted to reference head from within the department and are now supervising those who were former peers. As a library manager, your behavior and interactions must be above reproach and must set the standard for your staff. Ethical behavior, fairness, and integrity are essential characteristics now as they have always been. Trite as it may be, you must do the right thing, not just do things right.

DEVELOPING THE TALENT

It is the responsibility of the head of reference to bring together individuals with varying skills, personalities, and experience and develop them into a cohesive, collaborative, effective team. However, unlike an NFL coach, you cannot trade players to strengthen your team and eliminate weaknesses. But you can and must identify those areas that need to be strengthened, and as the manager, you must then determine how best to address that need. This is where the hiring process is so very critical. If you need someone with particular language skills, subject expertise, or teaching experience, you can specify those qualifications in a job posting. If, however, as is more likely the case, you do not have a vacancy to work with, then your own ingenuity must come into play. Is there someone in technical services who can provide language backup? Is there someone in access services or a branch who is interested in teaching? Creative collaboration across departmental lines cannot only solve your particular problem, but it can also develop a stronger, shared commitment within the organization to the library's goals.

Managing professionals requires a delicate touch. Reference librarians are often not onsite; in addition to working on the reference desk, they are teaching, meeting with faculty, working with students, preparing classes, developing reference guides, attending academic lectures or professional conferences, participating in meetings, and monitoring 24/7 reference lines. Librarians are a well-educated and highly dedicated group of individuals, and as a rule, they do not appreciate or operate well by being ordered to do something. They do, however, generally respond very well to a collaborative approach to management and decision-making. This does not remove the authority for making decisions from the manager, but the wise reference head will seek input, encourage discussion, and explain decisions fully. When widely divergent opinions emerge, the reference head must exercise strong yet subtle negotiation skills to bring the staff to a position of agreement and support. Conflict can be healthy by allowing different perspectives to be voiced, discussed, and evaluated, but the reference head must make the final decision and must do so in an atmosphere of openness.

THE LARGER ACADEMIC WORLD

The reference head's management skills must include far more than managing people. With the volatility of electronic resources and the increasingly virtual nature of the relationship among faculty and students and the library, remaining alert to any changes in the wind is critical. You must understand how the reference operation fits into the library as a whole and similarly how the library fits into the broader academic institution. Likewise, the mission of the reference department must mesh with and support those of the library and the university. The library is not just a support service; the library is an integral part of the institution and must contribute to the academic program. In order to do so, the library must understand and be active in the life of the organization. The reference head must seek out partnerships with faculty and other administrators and must identify and capitalize on opportunities to integrate the library more fully into the programs of the university. By being plugged into the academy, the reference head will be able to anticipate programmatic changes in the curriculum and research and make appropriate adjustments in staffing, services, and collections.

As a middle manager, the head of reference must not only recognize and value the integrated nature of library operations across departments but must also understand that it is not possible to separate units from one another. To paraphrase Vince Lombardi, intra-library collaboration is not just good, is not just essential; it is the only way. However, developing those cross-unit relationships requires trust, openness, and a willingness to negotiate and compromise for the good of the library as a whole. And that will take time.

CHANGE AND HUMAN NATURE

Change is inevitable if the organization is to survive. As a library manager, you must find the balance between healthy change and too much stress. Librarians are by nature intellectually curious, and most enjoy exploring possibilities and testing new ideas and approaches. However, too much change at one time can be threatening. As a library manager, you must demonstrate your steadiness, vision, and courage so that your staff can feel comfortable and follow your lead. Perfection can no longer be a reasonable goal, but quality is. As the head of reference, you cannot allow yourself and your department to drown in routine; you must lead them above it and ride the wave. Help your staff to find ways to break free from established, but perhaps no longer efficient, procedures. Encourage vision and leadership, and reward new approaches.

Library administration can state the mission and set the larger vision, but they cannot make it happen. Middle managers make it happen, and it is your responsibility to manage up as well as down. It is critical to make your arguments clearly and persuasively in order to effectively share your perspectives with the library administration.

Traditional reference activities are changing. Our users still seek information, but they want it immediately, and they want it on their desktops. Over-the-reference-desk transactions will continue, but, as most libraries have already seen, they will occur less frequently. Yet even as most academic libraries are finding that the reference questions are fewer, those questions tend to be more complex and indicate that students and faculty have frequently used Web resources to explore research directions or to search for pertinent material before coming to the library.

Individual consultations between a faculty member or student and a research librarian will become more commonplace, resulting in professional relationships that will grow and develop. First year students who discover the value of having "their own" reference librarian will return again and again throughout their academic careers. They will learn the value of having someone other than peers or instructors to discuss ideas with, someone who knows about their discipline and how to find information about it, someone who can help them to focus their research. In addition to preparing library instruction for classes, librarians will work with individual users to probe more deeply into their research needs and help them to discover additional relevant resources and approaches.

With the vastly increasing amount of information becoming available on the Web, librarians will work more with faculty to discover and then to determine how best to integrate that information into the curriculum. Knowing that previously unavailable materials are now just a few clicks away can make a great difference in how a faculty member might craft his or her course. Librarians know how to stay on top of emerging research and newly digitized resources, and by partnering with faculty, we can be effective collaborators.

Working relationships between librarians and faculty are already strong in many academic institutions, but they must become more formally accepted as common practice and a basic part of the reference librarians' job responsibilities. These relationships are key to our continuing effectiveness and indeed to our survival, and the head of reference must foster the outreach by librarians that will create, maintain, and enhance such partnerships.

General academic strength is a given requirement for a reference librarian. However, in order to partner effectively with faculty, librarians must not only be skilled in identifying and using information, they must bring subject expertise to the table. While many librarians already have second master's degrees and doctorates, teaching expertise and knowledge, continuing education and/or advanced degrees will become increasingly necessary so that we can speak the same language as the faculty and establish our credibility. If we expect to have a greater role in the shaping of individual courses and the curriculum, if we want to participate more fully in the academy, we will need to have the credentials. It is important for the head of reference to encourage further graduate work for librarians and to seek relevant advanced degrees when hiring new librarians. In order for reference librarians to become more fully integrated into the life of the academy, it is especially necessary to be adept at teaching, whether in a classroom setting or one-on-one.

DOLLAR SIGNS

As both costs and budgetary pressures have increased, library resources–both human and collections–have suffered. Our users want and expect us to provide access to more electronic resources, but consolidation of publishers, bundling of serial titles, and more restrictive intellectual property rights make it difficult to provide that access at a reasonable cost. Dollars and what they can purchase are shrinking, and at the same time, union contracts and increasing fringe benefit rates put pressure on personnel budgets. As prudent library managers, we must assume that this is likely not a temporary scenario but rather the way things will be, and we must plan accordingly.

Budget planning used to be an annual exercise. Each year the head of reference was given a sum of money and had to determine how to expand and enhance services and collections or, if necessary, how and where to reduce costs without seriously hampering services. However, budgeting has become a year-round exercise, a regular part of the manager's routine. Costs fluctuate more widely and more often, mandates come from either the library or university administration that require adjustments to expenditures, and mid-year–or more frequent–alterations must be made to the budget. In order to be ready to respond to these demands, the head of reference must be more than a data collector; he or she must be a data analyst.

Reference librarians often resist being measured as they rightly argue that what they do cannot be fully understood in terms of tick marks on a sheet of paper. However, though quantitative analysis does not adequately explain what goes on in a reference department, the data do indicate the nature of use and service, the times when users have come to us, and how long we have spent on particular tasks. Should it be necessary to reduce hours of reference service, the number of reference librarians on the desk at any given time, or even eliminate a service altogether, these data will allow you to make informed and defensible decisions. Since we know that students do not tend to study or need our assistance during the traditional hours of library operation, how can we best utilize our limited resources to be available at other times? Should we be considering the use of 24/7 chat lines? Should we be scheduling our librarians differently? Should librarians be "on duty" while at home? The data will help to make the options clearer even if implementing the options pose other challenges. To meet student needs optimally will require very creative, and possibly unorthodox, schedules and services in the near future. It may be that job postings will read, "Must be available to work from home 9 to 5–that is, 9 p.m. to 5 a.m." If we follow to its logical conclusion the argument that the library needs to be highly responsive to its users, the greatest flexibility and creativity in meeting their needs must be in reference services.

Having vast amounts of information easily accessible electronically opens doors that, only two decades ago, we could barely imagine might exist. Many of us remember poring laboriously over small-print paper indexes and trying to convince reluctant, disbelieving students that it was worth the time, effort, and eye strain to discover the best resources. Now a few clicks can achieve the same–and often better–results. However, because it is relatively easy to create electronic avenues to information, more and more is available online–for a price. And since our users want more and more, saying "No" can be very difficult. Yet saying "No" may well be the responsible thing to do since it may allow for better use of the limited financial resources available to you. Just because we can, does not mean that we should.

MAKING THE CONNECTIONS

Sometimes heads of reference have been heard to wonder, "Why do I do this?" In fact, many managers have days when they ask themselves and others that question, but it seems to come up quite often in reference. I believe that this happens because most reference librarians on the front lines really do love their work; they are invested in it both professionally and personally. When a reference librarian takes a chance and goes into management, he or she is often making a big personal trade off and relinquishing something they love (frequent reference work) for something that they believe in (administering and leading a department with all the challenges, headaches, and responsibilities that entails).

But at those times of self-doubt or questioning, it may be useful to remind yourself of the reasons why you entered the field in the first place. Remember the intellectual curiosity that drew you into librarianship, the excitement of information discovery, the enjoyment of working with people, and the thrill of connecting researchers to the resources they need. And then remember that managing a reference department is all of this on a larger scale.

Being an effective head of reference requires exceptional management skills, but it still also requires being an exceptional librarian, and being both is as much of an art as it is a science. Understanding how knowledge is organized, how to search for and evaluate information, how to teach students and faculty, and how to relate one resource to another draws on imagination and creativity much more than on memory. Supporting, encouraging, challenging, and managing librarians who understand how to do these things and do them well is demanding, and the underlying skill that a head of reference must have is the ability to recognize relationships and make connections between concepts, among individuals, throughout the library, and around the campus. Having your life consist of making so many different connections can be stimulating, exhilarating, rewarding, and worthwhile.

Why *wouldn't* you want to do this?

NOTE

1. "Beware Blogging Blunders: Interview Tips for the Library Digital Age," *Library Journal*, September 15, 2002, no. 15, pp. 42-44.

From Core Competencies to Desired Traits: Hiring a Head of Reference for the New Millennium

Philip C. Howze

SUMMARY. Reference librarianship in academic libraries has entered into a new century, and the profession will need competent reference managers more than ever. Gone are the days when a reference librarian was promoted to head the reference department based on an interest in supervising others, longevity and experience. The number of applicants in search pools for head of reference positions continues to decline. As the demand for electronic products and other venues of convenience for information delivery continues to increase, the nature of reference practice will change to meet the needs of the user. Unless one prepares for it, that change will be involuntary. This paper examines some of the qualifications, or desired traits, librarians should have who are interested in head of reference positions. *[Article copies available for a fee from The Haworth Document Delivery Service: 1-800-HAWORTH. E-mail address: <docdelivery@haworthpress.com> Website: <http://www.HaworthPress.com> © 2003 by The Haworth Press, Inc. All rights reserved.]*

KEYWORDS. Heads of reference, core competencies, desired traits, academic libraries, supervisors, managers, public services

Philip C. Howze, MLS, MPA, is Social Sciences Librarian, Morris Library, Southern Illinois University at Carbondale, Mailcode 6632, Carbondale, IL 62901-6632 (E-mail: phowze@lib.siu.edu).

[Haworth co-indexing entry note]: "From Core Competencies to Desired Traits: Hiring a Head of Reference for the New Millennium." Howze, Philip C. Co-published simultaneously in *The Reference Librarian* (The Haworth Information Press, an imprint of The Haworth Press, Inc.) No. 81, 2003, pp. 17-33; and: *Managing the Twenty-First Century Reference Department: Challenges and Prospects* (ed: Kwasi Sarkodie-Mensah) The Haworth Information Press, an imprint of The Haworth Press, Inc., 2003, pp. 17-33. Single or multiple copies of this article are available for a fee from The Haworth Document Delivery Service [1-800-HAWORTH, 9:00 a.m. - 5:00 p.m. (EST). E-mail address: docdelivery@haworthpress.com].

10.1300/J120v39n81_03

On August 23, 2001, *The New York Times* reported that, according to the American Library Association, colleges and universities are turning out more library and information science graduates than ever, but [public] libraries must compete with the growing number of higher paying jobs in the private sector. At the same time, the need for public, school and academic librarians is growing (Fountain, 2001). Academic libraries are already feeling the pinch. With additional job requirements such as supervisory experience and many years of practitioner experience, there is an even greater shortage of qualified applicants for head of reference positions than ever before. There are more openings than there are applicants, according to ALA, and the biggest shortage is in the area of library administration (Fountain, p. A12).

When hiring a head of reference, particularly during a period when the demographics of academic librarianship are changing so radically, libraries need to look at different criteria than those traditionally sought for similar positions. Job requirements will shift from core or traditional competencies to desired traits. The profession will need to invest in new talent by actively recruiting librarians who, with sufficient time and training, will become competent and effective reference managers.

THE TRADITIONAL HEAD OF REFERENCE

The traditional head of reference was, and in many libraries still is, a combination of supervisor and lead practitioner. Supervision once was generally thought to mean continuous source training, practical observation, and written evaluation for and of less experienced librarians. Apprenticeship has been replaced, or complicated by, subject specialization, tenure and collective bargaining. In addition to supervision, the head of reference was expected to have other "core competencies" including years of reference practice, strong tertiary source knowledge and superior information-seeking skills.

For years, the lead or "head" reference librarian demonstrated expertise by tutoring new librarians in the use of reference sources. As reference sources grew in number, heads of reference became established as "managers" by effectively decentralizing housekeeping tasks, or "operationalizing" the reference department. Instead of answering patron questions using the once relatively small but mighty group of highly reliable sources kept behind the desk, "reference" became a full-fledged department with such components as reference operations, desk scheduling, and reference collection development.

Reference operations evolved into a sub-specialty when practice shifted to a process. Routine tasks such as shelving, marking and labeling, rotating the exam shelf, supervising student assistants, maintaining reference collection indexes and stacks directories, and stocking supplies became the domain of reference operations. In addition, the reference operations staff was responsible for replenishing handout racks and bookmark containers, along with a host of other duties.

Desk scheduling has become an art form. The need to accommodate scheduling conflicts for reference librarians persisted, in part, because of a number of factors, including the multiple demands of faculty status, equity of desk hours scheduled among practitioners, and other conflicts such as vacations, meetings, sick leave and personal appointments. Also complicating the scheduling process in some libraries is resistance, by a number of practitioners, to working on Sundays.

Reference collection development became a subspecialty because of a publishing surge in tertiary sources, once only found in print and now widely available in electronic formats. Critical decision-making concerning which of myriad reference tools to buy, as well as space concerns, including weeding, became very important considerations for the reference collection development staff.

As reference departments grew in size and operational complexity, heads of reference had to know how to practice and teach reference, as well as direct reference operations. Additionally, the Head of Reference had to be an experienced practitioner who had supervisory skills, and later had to develop managerial skills. Some issues related to these qualifications are now discussed, as the position has evolved in libraries.

EXPERIENCE AS A PRACTITIONER

There was a time when a reference practitioner moved into supervision, many of his or her fellow librarians thought that the person would become a "working" supervisor, a lead practitioner of a fashion, who would work a full share of desk hours like everyone else. It was also expected that, similar to the guild system, this person would at least be a journeyman if not a master reference librarian. Core competencies have changed. Kong (1996) describes some of the newer core competencies for academic reference librarians, including "a flexible attitude and approach toward technology, a high tolerance for rapid technological change, creativity, curiosity, communication skills, public relations savvy, and the ability to relate effectively to a diverse clientele."

Reference experience and a strong source repertoire (formerly in print sources) have been somewhat displaced by the Internet and a host of other constantly evolving electronic products which new librarians often are more familiar with than practitioners with longevity. Reference experience (question negotiation, reference interview) and systematic information seeking skills have also been replaced–with the distance education/service to remote users movement, the rise of "good enough" as a user-determined standard for information seeking, and the subsequent decline in reference mediation.

TRADING ONE SET OF SKILLS FOR ANOTHER: BECOMING A SUPERVISOR

When one changes jobs from practitioner to supervisor one often finds that he or she is trading one set of skills for another, and the trading period can be quite unsettling–particularly for new supervisors. Supervision generally means a step up, becoming the evaluator instead of the evaluated. Instead of doing the assigned work, the person now assigns the work. Instead of living up to a standard, the person now measures the work of others against that standard. These myths are generally shattered within the first two weeks. Supervising others gets easier with time and experience. The honeymoon, however, is a short one. This is why many job ads require previous supervisory experience; it is proof of the presence of a tough exterior. A number of librarians have supervised others, either formally or informally.

FORMAL versus INFORMAL SUPERVISION

Formal supervision is having the authority to assign, train, direct and evaluate the work of others. Informal supervision feels the same, although the circumstances tend to be voluntary. For example, when the head of reference asks an experienced librarian to train new librarians in the use of tertiary sources, the relationship between the experienced and new librarians is informal.

Another example is when reference librarians participate in collection development. They may receive their subject(s) and fund code assignment(s) from a "coordinator" without necessarily being evaluated by the person. The informal supervisor often does not have the authority to insist on practitioner compliance, and informal supervisory experience generally does not count when applying for a job as a head of reference. The formal supervisory experience requirement may be a major barrier to hiring new heads of reference.

SUPERVISORY EXPERIENCE AS A BARRIER TO HIRING

Supervisory experience as a formal job requirement can be a barrier to hiring new heads of reference for a couple of reasons. First, it is hard to obtain formal (legitimate) supervisory experience unless opportunities are created by the library's administration to "take a chance" on new talent by establishing supervisors-in-training programs or internships. Second, librarians can practice for a number of years, if not their entire careers, without ever having supervised anyone. As the national pool of applicants who have formal supervisory experience continues to dwindle, libraries are going to have to replenish the pool, so to speak. Third, a number of librarians have additional degrees in fields such as management, business, public and educational administration, and these individuals should not continue to go unnoticed when looking for supervisor trainees.

Experienced librarians who are highly assertive and express a desire to build their careers on an upward track should not be overlooked, either. The bottom line is that "previous supervisory experience" as a job requirement was used as an effective sifter to narrow the pool of applicants, just as an ALA accredited MLS was an effective sifter to narrow the pool in entry level positions. It is one that the profession can no longer afford. Also, an emerging issue, when hiring a head of reference, is what does the library really want–a supervisor or a manager?

SUPERVISION AS A BARRIER
TO EFFECTIVE MANAGEMENT

Heads of reference can be (and have been) either supervisors or managers, depending on the library's organizational size and structure. Supervisors and managers are not the same. Heads of reference who are hired to be managers will run into "role dissonance" if expected to perform too many supervisory tasks. Examples of supervisory tasks include making up the reference desk schedule, writing statistical reports, and training new librarians.

Supervision is a full-time job. Still, there are many libraries in which the head of reference, as supervisor, is also expected to work at the reference desk, develop collections, teach library instruction, and participate in outreach activities. There are a number of organizational models appropriate to managing units within universities, including libraries—depending on what one can afford (Becher, 1984). Smaller academic libraries may only be able to afford a flat structure of functional units, with the head of reference acting as a supervisor. In such a structure, the library director would be considered the manager, with considerable, centralized authority and budget responsibility.

The head of reference hired as a manager, however, will have a full plate of unique tasks that are different from those of the supervisor. Examples include: influencing the overall policy-making process of the library, setting department goals, planning for new library services, and serving at the pleasure of the dean or director, which will include a large measure of library governance. Supervision is only one part of the manager's repertoire, and participating in areas of professional practice will likely be out of the question.

One of the difficulties related to the head of reference position, and whether the person is to be in the role of supervisor or manager, is the need to decide which role is responsible for morale and work climate. When it comes to reference librarians, there is a clear relationship between practitioner morale and the quality of service delivery (Lowenthal, 1990). The rapport librarians have with their heads of reference is a very important factor in job satisfaction for either party. Also, reference-based programs such as library instruction tend to engender greater commitment from the library as a whole when those programs are managed directly by reference department heads instead of coordinators (Blazek, 1985).

Because these issues of morale and work climate are so important, and because it is far from clear whether the head of reference as supervisor, or the head as manager, should address them, library management as a whole needs to be supportive of the idea of promoting job satisfaction. Organizational changes, particularly those arising from strategic reengineering, often start with shifting managers, whose responsibilities change as the units they supervise change (Bloss and Lanier, 1997). The head of reference will have to resolve a number of complaints ranging from interpersonal disputes to printer problems.

Morale issues will drag a once-good manager back to acting like a front line supervisor if he or she lets them. Free consultation and therapy should be replaced with meaningful work and measurable outcomes. As individuals perform to a standard of excellence, if he or she is so motivated, they will feel good about themselves. Instead of agonizing over whether to hire an effective person who meets all of the core requirements, library administrators need to change the language of the job advertisement to interview people who may have certain desired traits.

DESIRED TRAITS

Search committees need to begin to look for desired traits, particularly when librarians who meet core requirements are in short supply. Traits, or social characteristics, are much more reliable over time than ill-placed workers who are asked to be or do something that they are not or do not enjoy. For the right person, being a head of reference can be very rewarding. Boden (1994) studied perceptions of library faculty members and found six categories of perceived roles (or traits) for library department heads: advocate, communicator, counselor, leader, manager, and motivator. For each category, strategies were identified that heads could implement to better serve their faculty's needs. It may be that, because of these complex and multiple roles, otherwise experienced people do not apply for jobs as head of reference.

Libraries need to begin to look for enduring qualities in people instead of a "been there, done that" listing of qualifications. If not, then the end result will likely be that search committees will receive some great résumés belonging to some lousy candidates.

The requirements to be an effective head of reference are already changing. Search committees should look for desired traits, "desired" because by articulating those qualities or characteristics of value to the library a litmus test is created against which a candidate can receive flexible consideration based on potential. The following traits are presented not for what they are, but for what they illustrate in terms of changing the library's thinking about the head of reference position.

Desired Traits for New Heads of Reference

Skills and/or education in collegial management

Reference experience in more than one library

Understanding of service quality and how it is measured

Open and honest receptivity to cultural diversity

Awareness of trends affecting both librarianship and higher education

Ability to direct the work of highly educated people

Sullivan (1992) examined the changing role of the middle manager or department head in research libraries, and identified a number of skills and abilities for effective management, as well as the need for continuing leadership training. A need for new position criteria is indicated, starting with a collegial management style.

COLLEGIAL MANAGEMENT

It is not uncommon to see the phrase "collegial management style" in current job ads for head of reference positions. This is one of those you'll-know-it-when-you-see-it type attributes, like interpersonal communication skills. Similar to a jar of spaghetti sauce where one finds the words "flavored with meat," collegial management is often intended to imply "flavored" with shared governance.

Collegial management is not a leaderless model. The leader is the person considered as first among equals. Among academic vice presidents, this person would likely be the provost. Success stories using this model are relatively few, which is interesting because the benefits are purported to be numerous (Erskine-Cullen, 1995). The authority base, for the collegial manager, comes not from legitimate power (the ability to hire, fire, define job content and direct the work of others) but from an ability to lead by persuasion, charisma and example. Success, for the collegial manager, means getting others to buy into change.

There are three assumptions underlying the collegial management model. First, all participants want to be actively involved in decision-making processes affecting their work. Second, all participants are capable of working in a milieu of ambiguity where formal rules often do not exist. Third, all participants are willing to work through the governance process in ways that are in the best interests of the group's mission. Collegial management may be articulated, then, as a trust-based management style that requires high worker participation in order to be effective.

Heads of reference should also be able to exist in, and manage, their departments in a style that is perceived as collegial by others. Problems can occur when the three assumptions listed above fail to be consistently reliable. It is not uncommon for the reference manager to be confronted with saboteurs, unhappy people who will act to derail any idea unless it is their own. There will be employees who do not want to do anything "extra" including becoming involved in workplace decision making. Also, there are library staff who simply cannot function without a clearly defined set of guidelines–but woe be unto the manager who writes them; that's not being collegial. Also, there are those workers who, after being awarded tenure, turn into "tenure terrorists" who refuse to support anything based on little more than general principles. Collegial management can be fraught with stress for the head of a faculty unit in such areas as time management, collegial confrontation, organizational constraints and academic productivity (Gmelch and Burns, 1990).

The collegial manager, because she or he is in fact first among equals, runs the ever-present risk of confrontation. Candor is often the payoff of collegial management; it is trust at work in the environment. Change, using the collegial management style, will be much slower than a directive approach (Croll and Abbott, 1994).

Collegial management is working when the reference manager is actively engaged in roles other than boss: mediator, advocate, provocateur, information broker, and part-time social worker. In short, effective collegial management is complex and chaotic because it is less concerned with individual people and personnel issues, and more concerned with cultivating an environment in which many things may live–including new knowledge, creativity, fear, hope and reasoned response to change. Sharing a knowledge base does not a colleague make–sharing ideas and a sense of culture also plays a part.

Financial constraints may also force libraries to engage in such techniques as subject specialization and collegial management (Altmann, 1988). One library attempted collegial management in its purest form: supervisory rotation by librarians taking turns on a two year cycle serving as department head (Perdue and Piotrowski, 1986).

Shared governance, as a tenant of collegial management, is possible if steps are taken to strengthen the shared governance process, and the faculty does not "give over" power through administrative centralization and its own provincialism, and the faculty becomes more involved in union affairs and becomes politically knowledgeable (Baldridge, 1982). There is the potential, however, for collegial management to prove successful in libraries (Bechtel, 1981), if the culture understands and is receptive to its complex nature and inherent hard work. Continuing education in management, particularly in the area of collegial management, could improve our outlook for future applicants (Wittenbach et al., 1992).

REFERENCE EXPERIENCE IN MORE THAN ONE LIBRARY

There is a "that's the way we've always done it" mentality that has had a crippling effect on libraries, public services departments in particular. This can be very harmful when the service model adopted by a given library is, or has the potential to be, more expensive than the library can afford to employ effectively. Some libraries, for example, employ the divisional model of reference.

The divisional model was supposed to do three things: promote ease of library use by the patron, continue the process of shelving like material together in the same contiguous area, and provide reference service for materials housed in the division. In main libraries of public library systems, it is very common to see this model, with collection separation by broad subject categories (Art and Humanities, Business Science and Technology, etc.). Its purpose was to cope with collection growth. Other libraries employ the subject specialist model.

The subject specialist, or liaison model was supposed to continue what the divisional model started, with the exception being that a librarian would now be responsible for each subject for which the university had a teaching or other programmatic interest. Also, the librarian, as subject specialist, would now get to participate in the "privilege" of selecting books and other materials. More decentralized than the divisional model, the subject specialist approach also had one purpose: to cope with collection growth. The more decentralized the model, the more it costs. There are a number of models, including tiered reference.

The reference manager must be familiar with a number of models, as well as be able to advocate for the most appropriate one based on availability of resources. No one model is necessarily better, or worse, than another; the question is, what can the library afford? While the opportunity to change the model of reference does not happen that often, lesser adjustments to services frequently occur, including the addition of new products and services. This is a matter of technique not to be overlooked or taken lightly.

Every change affects the overall service environment. One could simplistically observe that no library ever changed the way reference was practiced as a condition of employment when hiring a new librarian (or a head of reference, for that matter). No library ever changed its aggregator product subscription(s) as a condition of employment when hiring a new librarian, either.

Work experience in more than one library may give the head librarian a visceral perspective that there is no "one best way" to run a service point, and that a number of libraries do things differently. This flexibility of thought is imperative for the new reference manager, similar to knowing about certain reference sources despite their absence from the local collection. If it is not possible to glean this trait from the résumé, the search committee should examine for it, anyway. Some candidates come by flexibility of thought quite naturally, or as a result of personal experiences.

UNDERSTANDING LIBRARY SERVICE QUALITY

Quality in library service will be the hallmark of the future head of reference. A knowledge of, or familiarity with, LIBQUAL, libraries' adaptation of SERVQUAL, will serve the head of reference well in measuring service quality. According to Cook and Thompson (2000), SERVQUAL (developed in 1988 by Parasuraman, Berry, and Zeithaml) measured perceptions of service quality, originally in the retailing sector. Libraries and other educational institutions also began to see themselves as service providers. Librarians in particular have increasingly become interested in measuring quality of service as the ultimate assessment of library performance.

Measuring service quality means gauging the service expectation level, and the perceived level of service received, from the user's standpoint. The goal then, is to correct the discrepancy, or gap, between the two. Farrell (1998) discusses serving library patron needs in terms of customer service and quality control. Coleman et al. (1997) add to the discussion of measuring service quality in terms of tangibles (appearance of facilities, equipment, personnel, and communication materials), reliability, responsiveness, assurance, and empathy. Discrepancies between expectations and perceptions were found in reliability, responsiveness, assurance, and empathy.

Nitecki (1996) investigated how applicable SERVQUAL was to academic libraries and how influential the findings of such a study might be in changing what library administrators believe about the management of academic library services. Once again, this is based on gap theory, or the space between customer expectations and perceived service quality.

Heads of reference are agents of service quality. They are constantly looking for ways to improve what has long been accepted as a quality service, putting individuals in touch with the information they seek.

RECEPTIVITY TO CULTURAL DIVERSITY

Another important and enduring quality that a head of reference must have is an open and honest receptivity to cultural diversity. Jennings (1993) has presented widely in the area of cultural diversity in libraries. A number of variables have been considered in her work, including the following:

Jennings' Variables, Library Cultural Diversity

Effects of cultural diversity on academic libraries and library and information science education

Impact of demographics on affirmative action recruitment

Effects of demographic trends on library and information science professions, faculty attitudes

Library and information science curriculum and literature

Fitzgerald and Jones (1997) developed a special SPEC Kit describing the ARL Partnerships Program, created to enhance diversity in research libraries and allied associations. The goal was to actively engage more libraries and library-related organizations in advancing diversity initiatives. Creating a climate for diversity in libraries involves strategic planning, recruitment and retention activities, on-going educational programs, and consistent organizational assessment and adjustment.

The head of reference must have a wide perspective, as well as an interest in a number of subjects. The person must be on the side of intellectual freedom, and not be afraid to study the literature and customs of other cultures. The head of reference must be vigilant to make sure that racism does not have a chance to germinate, either overtly or covertly, when hiring librarians of color. The person must continue to advocate for a diverse practitioner base, in order to break down language barriers and technical barriers to patron success. In short, the head of reference must work to create and maintain what Jennings terms "a welcoming environment." In matters of personnel, libraries must seek, hire and retain a critical mass of librarians from among protected classes, so that library patrons can actually see the welcome mat.

AWARENESS OF TRENDS

An awareness of trends, or knowledge of how to find information on trends in librarianship, will be a great asset in the person hired as a head of reference. New services, new software, new electronic products, how statistics are kept, user preferences, consortial behavior, and personnel matters are very important things with which one should keep up. Examples of trends found in library literature include the future of the virtual university (Stalling, 2000); jargon and its impact on humanistic expression related to libraries (Candido, 1999); librarianship as an aging profession (Wilder, 1999); professionalism and the future of librarianship (Abbott, 1998); and the political economy of knowledge, of which libraries are but a part (Winter, 1996).

The benefit to the library that hires such a person is the intellectual connection with other libraries, which gives the local library setting context, whether on a state or national level. Questions rise from knowing library trends, including: How is this library doing, compared to others? How is this library doing, compared to its peer group? Is the library spending its money similarly to other libraries? Are reference departments buying fewer tertiary sources in print and more in electronic format? Which ones?

Knowledge of trends keeps a library connected to the rest of the world, which can be very helpful when setting standards for professional practice in reference. The head of reference should know something about the history of reference as a service, as well as reference theory, the transactional analysis of information seeking behavior, and the many roles of the reference librarian in affecting a satisfactory resolution to the information need.

DIRECTING THE WORK OF HIGHLY EDUCATED PEOPLE

Lastly, it will be important for the head of reference to acquire, in a relatively short period of time, the ability to direct the work of reference practitioners. It is not easy to direct the work of highly educated people. In fact, the "directing" only happens when there is a high degree of trust, or when outcomes are based on rational criteria. Rational models assume that people will behave in ways that represent their own best interests. Therefore, any attempt to direct the work of the faculty must answer the "whiifm" question: what's in it for me? This requires training. The need for training has been previously discussed in the literature (Wittenbach, 1992). Coaching can have a positive impact on seasoned professionals. It assumes that practitioner skills are no longer at issue, in the evaluative sense; but that there is an ongoing need for stimulation that can occur through exposure to interesting people, books, ideas and new developments in the field. Effective staff development programs can positively affect the work of highly educated people. Encouraging scholarship and service is also a part of directing the work of librarians, particularly those with faculty status. Coursework and/or practical training in teaching and/or supervision can also be helpful in this regard.

Professionals like ideas and techniques that will make their work easier, less, more interesting, or more effective. Professionals will willingly work for power, prestige and/or a sense of gratification that comes from helping others. One can expect a substantial amount of candor when working with highly educated people, particularly if they happen to be highly actualized as well. Experience is a great equalizer in power struggles; there will always be someone who knows more, or different things than the head–and if the librarian wants to really let the head of reference "have it," all she or he has to do is refuse to share knowledge.

One can also expect to struggle with the "whose side are you on?" question when library management and the reference department expect separate advocates. Also, there is a "fair share" expectation that the head of reference will also be on the desk schedule, including nights and weekends. Everyone will want something from the head of reference. Perhaps these things, and others, discourage seasoned practitioners from applying for such positions. If reference librarians are not careful in their treatment of the department head, then the day may come, very soon, when civilian managers, sans MLS, will run reference departments, and librarians will end up reporting to them. Now, would that be so bad?

Perhaps not. Non-MLS professionals run our personnel departments, manage our budgets, and handle a substantial number of our access services operations, including circulation and interlibrary loan, and run our systems departments. When library administrators are pressed to find leaders instead of lead librarians in order to carry out the overall mission of the library, then it may not be implausible to find administrative "directorships" in the organizational chart, with librarians reporting to them in the not too distant future.

CONCLUSION

As librarianship prepares for baby boomer retirements, the profession will need competent reference managers more than ever. The demand for electronic products and information delivery venues continues to increase, and reference practice is now more complex than ever. Instead of "core competencies" once believed that every head of reference should have, the profession needs to begin to look at desired traits, those qualities a lead reference practitioner should have that have the potential to stimulate quality reference service delivery. Focusing on desired traits promotes the likelihood of selecting a person with enduring capacities, instead of interviewing qualified, but poorly fitting candidates. It is time to take a chance on newcomers to management. The profession needs to look at librarians with new abilities instead of traditional core requirements. These abilities include skills and/or education in collegial management, public service experience in more than one library, a quality service orientation, open and honest receptivity to cultural diversity, knowledge of trends affecting both librarianship and higher education, and the ability to direct the work of highly educated people. Libraries can and must respond to the shortage of qualified leaders by establishing training programs and encouraging continuing education in management studies.

REFERENCES

Abbott, Andrew. (1998). "Professionalism and the Future of Librarianship," *Library Trends* 46 (Winter), 430-43.

Altmann, Anna E. (1988). "The Academic Library of Tomorrow: Who Will Do What?" *Canadian Library Journal* 45 (June), 147-52.

Baldridge, J. Victor. (1982). "Shared Governance: A Fable About the Lost Magic Kingdom," *Academe* 68 (January/February), 12-15.

Becher, Tony. (1984). "Principles and Politics: An Interpretative Framework for University Management," *International Journal of Institutional Management in Higher Education* 8 (November), 191-99.

Bechtel, Joan. (1981). "Collegial Management Breeds Success," *American Libraries* 12 (November), 605-607.

Blazek, Ron. (1985). "Effective Bibliographic Instruction Programs: A Comparison of Coordinators and Reference Heads in ARL Libraries," *RQ* 24 (Summer), 433-41.

Bloss, Alex and Don Lanier. (1997) "The Library Department Head in the Context of Matrix Management and Reengineering." *College and Research Libraries* 58 (November), 499-508.

Boden, Dana W. R. (1994). *A University Libraries Faculty Perspective on the Role of the Department Head in Faculty Performance: A Grounded Theory Approach, Revised.* (Eric Document Reproduction Service, ED377 758).

Candido, Anne Marie. (1999). "Fabricating and Prefabricating Language: Troubling Trends in Libraries," *Journal of Academic Librarianship* 25 (November), 433-38.

Coleman, Vicki, Yi Xiao, Linda Bair, and Bill Chollett. (1997). "Toward a TQM Paradigm: Using SERVQUAL to Measure Library Service Quality." *College and Research Libraries* 58 (May), 237-45; 248-51.

Cook, Colleen, and Bruce Thompson. (2000). *Higher-Order Factor Analysis as a Score Validity Evaluation Tool: An Example with a Measure of Perceptions of Library Service Quality.* (Eric Document Reproduction Service, ED438 312).

Croll, Paul, and Dorothy Abbott. (1994). *Coercion or Compromise: How Schools React to Imposed Change.* (Eric Document Reproduction Service, ED372 477).

Erskine Cullen, Ethne. (1995). "School-University Partnerships as Change Agents: One Success Story," *School Effectiveness and School improvement:* 6(3) 192-204.

Farrell, Maggie. (1998). "Quality Management and Building Government Information Services," *Government Information Quarterly* 15 (1) 89-91.

Fitzgerald, Allyn, and DeEtta Jones, eds. (1997). *ARL Partnerships Program: Breaking Down Walls and Building Bridges.* SPEC Kit 225. (Eric Document Reproduction Service, ED410 964).

Fountain, John. (2001), "Librarians Adjust Image in an Effort to Fill Jobs," *The New York Times*, (August 23, 2001, late edition), A12.

Gmelch, Walter H. and John S. Burns. (1990). *The Cost of Academic Leadership: Department Chair Stress.* (Eric Document Reproduction Service, ED 341 146).

Jennings, Kriza A. (1993). "Recruiting New Populations to the Library Profession," *Journal of Library Administration* 19 (3-4) 175-91.

Kong, Leslie M. (1996). "Academic Reference Librarians: Under the Microscope," *The Reference Librarian* 54, 21-27.

Lowenthal, Ralph A. (1990). "Preliminary Indications of the Relationship between Reference Morale and Performance," *RQ* 29 (Spring), 380-93.

Nitecki, Danuta A. (1996). "Changing the Concept and Measure of Service Quality in Academic Libraries," *Journal of Academic Librarianship* 22 (May), 181-90.

Perdue, Bob, and Chris Piotrowski. (1986). "Supervisory Rotation: Impact on an Academic Library Reference Staff," *RQ* 25 (Spring), 361-65.

Stalling, Dees. (2000). "The Virtual University, Legitimized at Century's End: Future Uncertain for the New Millennium," *Journal of Academic Librarianship* 26 (January), 3-14.

Sullivan, Maureen. (1992). "The Changing Role of the Middle Manager in Research Libraries," *Library Trends* 41 (Fall), 269-81.

Wilder, Stanley J. (1999). "The Age Profile of Librarianship," *Journal of Library Administration* 28 (3) 5-14.

Winter, Michael F. (1996). "Specialization, Territoriality, and Jurisdiction: Librarianship and the Political Economy of Knowledge," *Library Trends* 45 (Fall), 343-63.

Wittenbach, Stefanie A., Sever M. Bordeianu and Kristine Wycisk. (1992). "Management Preparation and Training of Department Heads in ARL Libraries," *College and Research Libraries* 53 (July), 319-30.

Managing the 21st Century Reference Department: Competencies

Justina O. Osa

SUMMARY. The reference department of the 21st century has to provide services, which are constantly being shaped by the changes in the information environment and the expectations of patrons of the fast-paced era. The presence of a visionary and dynamic leader to direct and influence the behaviors and activities of the staff who must provide the reference services is an important component in the delivery of quality services. This article focuses on the competencies that the leader must possess in order to get the job done well and influence and direct the employees' abilities towards the achievement of the department's predetermined goals. Some of the core competencies considered valuable for the reference leader are identified, defined and discussed. *[Article copies available for a fee from The Haworth Document Delivery Service: 1-800-HAWORTH. E-mail address: <docdelivery@haworthpress.com> Website: <http://www. HaworthPress.com> © 2003 by The Haworth Press, Inc. All rights reserved.]*

Justina O. Osa, BA, MSLS, MEd, EdD, is Education and Behavioral Sciences Librarian, The Pennsylvania State University, University Libraries, Education & Behavioral Sciences Library, E-502C Paterno, University Park, PA 16802 (E-mail: joo2@ psu.edu).

[Haworth co-indexing entry note]: "Managing the 21st Century Reference Department: Competencies." Osa, Justina O. Co-published simultaneously in *The Reference Librarian* (The Haworth Information Press, an imprint of The Haworth Press, Inc.) No. 81, 2003, pp. 35-50; and: *Managing the Twenty-First Century Reference Department: Challenges and Prospects* (ed: Kwasi Sarkodie-Mensah) The Haworth Information Press, an imprint of The Haworth Press, Inc., 2003, pp. 35-50. Single or multiple copies of this article are available for a fee from The Haworth Document Delivery Service [1-800-HAWORTH, 9:00 a.m. - 5:00 p.m. (EST). E-mail address: docdelivery@haworthpress.com].

KEYWORDS. Leading, managing, competencies, reference department, 21st century

Why did dinosaurs become extinct? They failed to change with their environment.

–Gregory P. Smith

INTRODUCTION

The 21st century is seen as the era of electronic generation and as an era of constant change. The environment in which reference services are provided has drastically changed and is still changing. Patron expectations have changed dramatically by the advent and continuous invasion of new technologies in the information arena. Today, most of library patrons expect stellar, quick-response service from the library. The reference desk is primarily concerned with answering questions from physically present patrons and virtual patrons.

"The academic library of the 21st century is an institution facing numerous challenges, both from within and from without. Change is constant and everywhere."[1] In the 21st century, the set of challenges and demands the reference department leader must navigate are different from those of the previous era. This set of challenges and demands requires a whole different set of answers. Library personnel of necessity need new ways of thinking. The reference leader cannot expect success either by leading today using yesterday's methods, or using yesterday's roadmap to navigate today's roads.

Beckhard states that there is an increasing awareness that people are the key factor in organizational effectiveness in the 21st century.[2] The reference department cannot offer the expected exceptional service without outstanding frontline staff on the reference desk. The presence of strong, visionary, and effective leadership is a crucial component of the successful reference department. In the 21st century, the head of the reference department will need to exhibit a set of behaviors that are far different from the ones of the previous era. For the reference department leader to provide adequate leadership that would guarantee quality reference services, he/she has to have certain managerial and leadership competences in his/her repertoire. These sets of knowledge and skills are usually related to focusing on getting the job done and focusing on establishing a workplace where employees are committed to excellence in a changing environment.

This article focuses on the competencies that the leader must possess in order to get the job done well and influence the employees' behaviors to enable the department to achieve its predetermined goals. These competencies are the building blocks representing the core understanding and capabilities required of an effective reference department leader. Some of the core competencies considered valuable for the reference leader, which are identified, defined, and discussed include: (1) creating and communicating a vision, mission, and goal(s), (2) creating and maintaining a positive and nurturing workplace climate and culture, (3) setting expectations, (4) being task-centered and employee-centered, (5) motivating, (6) delegating, (7) communicating, and (8) staffing.

DEFINITIONS

Leading and Managing

"Leadership is a combination and application of personal traits, knowledge, skills, talents, attitudes and abilities . . . "[3] There is a difference in the concepts of leading and managing. Leading implies the ability to set direction and to influence the behaviors of others toward the attainment of a predetermined goal or set of goals. It is doing the right thing. Managing is preoccupation with structures and procedures. It is doing the thing right. "Management is not bad and leadership good. Both are needed."[4] While leading focuses primarily on people, managing focuses primarily on the task to be completed. Leadership and managing thus become the two sides of the coin. An ideal situation arises when there is a good blend of both.

Competencies

Competencies are the combination of knowledge, skills, and abilities which are relevant in a particular job position and which, when acquired, allow a person to perform a task or function at a high level of proficiency. Woodruffe, in his article "What Is Meant by Competency" defines a competency as "a set of behavior patterns that the incumbent needs to bring to a position in order to perform its tasks and functions with competence."[5]

LITERATURE REVIEW

"Reference librarianship has changed tremendously in the last twenty years."[6] Libraries are facing incredible constant change, greater demand for accountability, and a higher level of performance. The reference department has undergone and is still undergoing changes. Some libraries have had to restructure the library organization and in the process have combined circulation, readers' services and reference together as a single unit. Others have added the interlibrary loan and document delivery to their reference department. New technologies are affecting the way the reference department performs its duties because "technology is dramatically changing library practices and procedures. More significantly, technology is changing user expectations."[7]

Another major change is the staffing of the reference desk. There used to be a time in the history of the library when only professional librarians staffed the reference desk. Due to budgetary constraints, paraprofessionals now staff the reference desk in many libraries. It is therefore not surprising that there is a high interest in the concept of effective leadership in the library. The leader has to find ways to enhance the quality of the performance of all the employees he/she has, and influence their behaviors so that patrons will receive high level reference services.

As Peter Northouse noted, "Leadership has become a highly popular topic."[8] The literature on leadership is very extensive. Leadership is a concept that has intrigued humans. Though it could be very evasive we know it when we see it. "First, leadership is a relationship between two or more people in which influence and power are unevenly distributed."[9] There are, of course, as many styles of leadership as there are leaders because we are all individuals who lead in our own unique ways. On the other hand there are certain behaviors and competencies of our leadership style that we can make a conscious decision about in order to help us influence the group or unit we lead into success. The peculiar characteristics of the library of the 21st century place a heavy burden, huge demand and high responsibility on the reference department staff who are the frontline library staff. The leader for today and the future will benefit from works that focus on "*how to be*–how to develop quality, character, mind-set, principles, and courage."[10] If the reference department employees are to succeed in a fast-paced, information-hungry environment, and in a time of accountability and rapid change, the reference department must have a new type of leader who possesses certain competencies. Such competencies that have the potential to enhance the effectiveness of the reference department leader to be task-focused, and people/employee-focused, are discussed below.

CREATING AND COMMUNICATING A VISION, MISSION AND GOAL(S)

Would you tell me, please, said Alice, which way I ought to walk from here? That depends a good deal on where you want to get to, said the cat.

–Carroll, 1941

These two sentences above, pretty well state the crucial role vision, mission, and goals play in directing and in focusing every activity an individual or a group or an institution undertakes when there is an outcome/product expected. The reference department leader first and foremost needs to develop and communicate a vision, mission, philosophy and goal of the department. The reference department often becomes the lengthened shadow of its leader. He/she must be a visionary, must have a mental picture of what the department should be, must have a dream and must believe in the beauty of that dream. Vision is the thoughtful future analysis and planning that enables leaders to develop a system to forecast the future. Vision should help answer three questions:

1. Where are we going?
2. How will we get there?
3. How will we know when we have arrived?

It should represent achievable, challenging, and worthwhile long-range and short-range goals to which staff can direct their energies. Leaders look further into the future than their employees. They envision what needs to be accomplished and influence their employees to complete great goals. The vision the leader has engenders a mission, which in turn enables the department to form its goal(s). The goal provides a sense of direction, a road map, and enhances unity of purpose among the staff. The goal-setting theory advocates for goals that are clear, well articulated, realistic, specific, attainable, challenging and reasonably measurable. The inscription on a church wall says it well:

A task without a vision is drudgery.
A vision without a task is but a dream.
But a vision with a task is the hope of the world.[11]

The leader has to communicate and share the vision, mission, and goals with every member of the staff. According to Senge, "The practice of shared vision involves the skills of unearthing shared 'picture of the future' that foster genuine commitment and enrollment rather than compliance."[12] Soliciting the input of employees into the development and fine-tuning of the vision, mission, and goals of the reference department will further enhance the success of the department. Employees will feel committed to goals they help develop and put forth required energy to achieve them. The leader can hope for the staff to buy into his/her vision, mission and goals when he/she is able to develop those that staff can endorse. Some of the advantages of shared vision, mission and goals include they:

1. Direct attention and action
2. Mobilize energy
3. Lead to higher effort
4. Increase persistent effort
5. Motivate staff to develop strategies that will enhance their performing at the required levels
6. Lead to goal attainment, which often leads to a high sense of satisfaction and positive self-worth and self-esteem, and further motivation to achieve even more.

CREATING AND MAINTAINING A POSITIVE AND NURTURING WORKPLACE CLIMATE AND CULTURE

A happy worker is a loyal and committed worker.

Leading is first and foremost a people business. Employees are often the most important resource of any organization. The department leader achieves "things" through the employees. Workplace climate could be defined as the collective perceptions by employees of what it feels like to be an employee in a particular department, where those perceptions influence employees' motivation to learn and perform to the best of their ability. The climate of the reference department helps to establish and sustain a motivated work environment that fosters commitment, esprit de corps, team spirit, pride, trust, and group identity. Organizational culture is the shared philosophies, expectations, attitudes, norms and values of the organization. William Ouchi's Theory Z addresses a culture and a way of life that exists at the organizational level. It advocates trust and loyalty to the organizational philosophy and goal that gives direction to organizational actions and provides meanings to organizational members.[13] The climate and the culture of the reference department play a critical role in the quality of the services provided to patrons. It is often unusual to find a reference department succeeding while the reference staff members are failing. The highest achievable level of service comes from the heart, so the department that reaches the employees' heart will provide the very best services to customers. When the climate and culture are such that employees feel valued, appreciated, celebrated, and respected, employees feel proud, connected and committed. The culminating result is a reference department with a winning climate where staff morale is high and where staff members are eager to go the extra mile to deliver high quality reference services to patrons.

Furthermore, the reference leader should acquire the competency to establish and maintain a workplace climate that is non-threatening, nurturing, supportive, and safe. Such a climate fosters staff creativity, risk-taking, and effectiveness. Leaders who rise above the level of mediocrity are often good at people skills. When a leader fails to establish and sustain a workplace where people are valued and where their emotional needs are met, he/she is begging for trouble. Things and stuff cannot plot, scheme, create, praise and share. But people can. An orderly, stress-free work environment promotes task-orientedness, which leads to goal attainment. Effectiveness can be further heightened when the leader listens to employees who often ask to be managed with H-E-A-R-T. This means:

H–Hear and understand me.

E–Even if you disagree with me please do not make me run.

A–Acknowledge the greatness in me.

R–Remember to look for my noble intention.

T–Tell me the truth with compassion.

Another factor that promotes positive workplace climate is good manners. Good manners are the lubricating oil of good relationships. Good manners and proper workplace etiquette should be maintained as much as possible at all times. Even when dealing with a difficult employee or situation the leader should not get angry, emotional, or try to get even. The leader should focus on managing the situation in such a way that he/she gets what he/she desires from that situation. The leader should keep his/her eyes on the prize. He/she should resist the temptation to jump to "Who is causing the problem?" and focus on "With whom is the problem happening?" Conflicts should be resolved in a positive and constructive manner. When there is a problem the reference leader should:

1. Define the problem
2. Look at potential causes of the problem
3. Identify alternatives for approaches to resolve the problem
4. Select the approach with the highest potential to resolve the problem
5. Design a plan to implement the best alternative
6. Monitor the implementation of the plan
7. Verify the efficacy of the plan in solving the problem.

Having a good sense of time prevents conflict and resistance. The leader should anticipate, identify, diagnose, and consult on potential or actual problems. He/she should know when to introduce changes and when to assign additional responsibilities to staff members.

Everyone likes to be "celebrated." The reference leader should seek ways to "celebrate" his/her staff. The leader should know his/her staff well enough to know how to reward them. He/she should think of new ways to transform his/her employees to winners and to come up with innovative and creative ways to reward and energize them. It does not have to be expensive or monetary. Rewards could be in the form of:

1. A thank you note
2. A verbal affirmation such as "Wow that was just terrific!"
3. A free lunch (there is something about free lunch that wins faithful and loyal employees for the leader)
4. A cheap card
5. A genuine compliment paid to deserving employees
6. An acknowledgement of staff strengths.

SETTING EXPECTATIONS

The difference between a lady and a flower girl is not how she behaves but how she's treated.

–Eliza Doolittle in George Bernard Shaw's *Pygmalion*

Typically, people behave in a way that is consistent with the expectations others have for them or those they have for themselves. This in brief, is the concept of the Pygmalion effect. Setting and communicating high expectations and high standard reference services for staff is one of the leader competencies that could boost effectiveness. The concept of the self-fulfilling prophecy can be summarized in these key principles:

- We form certain expectations of people or events.
- We communicate those expectations with various cues.
- People tend to respond to these cues by adjusting their behavior to match them.
- The result is that the original expectation becomes true.

This creates a circle of self-fulfilling prophecies.[14] Goble confirms the concept and states that support paraprofessionals tend to deliver what is expected.[15]

The view that the leader holds of people would generally influence how he/she sees his staff and how he/she treats them. The way many leaders treat employees is often a direct product of the assumptions they hold about people. These assumptions are presented under Theory X and Theory Y. Theory X leader believes that the average person: is lazy; has an inherent dislike of work; and will avoid it if he/she can. Furthermore, Theory X leader believes that most people must be coerced, controlled, directed, and threatened to get them to put forth adequate effort toward the attainment of organizational/unit goal(s).[16] Theory Y leader, on the other hand, believes that the average person: finds work as natural as play or rest; external control and threat of punishment are not the only means of bringing about effort towards organizational/unit goal(s) and will exercise self-direction and self-control in the service of objectives to which he/she is committed; and under the proper conditions will not only accept but seek responsibility.[17] The reference leader would lead the reference department of the 21st century more effectively if he/she develops and maintains a positive faith in the ability and predisposition of the staff. Leading, managing and supervising the staff should not degenerate to "snoopervision" or an episode of private "cold war."

Leaders who demand excellence of themselves and their staff enhance effectiveness. But the leader should set expectations that pass the test of reality and that can be translated into performance. It is only when employees are able to fulfill expectations, that each accomplishment can spur them on to higher peaks and challenge others to climb the same peaks and bask in the sunlight of success. Employees would understand and be more aware of the set expectations when the leader and the staff, whenever possible collaborate to:

1. Develop policies and procedures for the efficient operation of all reference functions and activities
2. Establish rules and regulations to guide staff behaviors
3. Schedule regular meetings
4. Develop an employee manual
5. Provide feedback–focus on the behavior rather than on the person
6. Maintain channels of communication such as a newsletter and weekly communiqué.

BEING TASK-CENTERED AND EMPLOYEE-CENTERED

Both the Ohio State Studies: Initiating Structure and Consideration; and the Michigan Studies: Production-Centered and Employee-Centered focus on identifying those leader behaviors that enhance the attainment of predetermined organizational goal(s). Leader behaviors could be grouped into two distinct clusters–task-centered behaviors and employee-centered behaviors. The leader who is task-centered focuses directly on setting tight work standards, organizing, defining and assigning task carefully, prescribing work methods to be followed, emphasizing meeting deadlines, closely supervising subordinates, and delineating relationships with staff members.[18] Such a leader makes sure that the staff members know exactly what the task and the expectation are. But the leader who is employee-centered exhibits trust, respect, warmth, support, and concern for the welfare of staff. He/she focuses on the development of interpersonal relationships, uses group decision-making, and endeavors to treat staff in a sensitive and considerate way.[19] Such a leader enhances psychological closeness between him/herself and the staff members and reaches their heart. The staff members tend to become eager to give their all to attain the highest achievable level of reference service to patrons, and have a passion for each patron's success. For effectiveness, the reference leader should focus on both the task-centered and employee-centered dimensions of leadership. None should be sacrificed for the other because a good combination of both dimensions is ideal for leadership in the 21st century.

MOTIVATING

Motivation can be defined as that force or that drive within the employee that moves him/her to direct his/her behaviors, energies and efforts toward the attainment of the predetermined goal(s) of the reference department. The leader needs to be mindful of the application of basic psychology to his/her interaction with the staff. All human actions are motivated. Staff members do things or fail to do things for their own reasons. As Abraham Maslow observed, man is an animal always in a state of needs. His need hierarchy theory supports the belief that the moment a lower level need is met, a higher level need exhibits itself, and until the lower level need is satisfied a higher level need will not be attained.[20] The reference leader should aim at enabling employees to move up the five levels of needs–physiological, safety, social, esteem, and self-actualization, until they attain self-fulfillment or self-actualization. Riggs and Sykes confirm that the leader should make followers feel good about themselves, support the deepest psychological needs of followers, make employees feel they are doing a good job and give them recognition for it.[21] Ultimately the goal of motivation is performance. Recognition of staff contributions is a vital motivating factor. The reference leader should be liberal with his/her positive reinforcement and rewards. He/she must not give praise as if he/she is reaching into his/her wallet. Employees should be rewarded in ways that they see as reward. Remember that reward could be personal because what is a reward for one staff member could be punishment to another.

The reference leader should develop and refine his/her participatory leadership skill. He/she should encourage the entire staff to think "outside of the box." Creativity and initiative are to be encouraged and rewarded.[22] The leader should encourage the staff to think, solicit their input, and whenever appropriate use feedback from staff. Employees should never be made to feel that they need to leave their brains at the front door of the library and pick them up at the end of the workday. Followers become de-motivated when they see themselves as "choiceless doers" forced to carry our rules, regulations, and organizational charts.[23] But when they are involved in the decision-making process, they have a sense of belonging and of importance, they feel committed to make the decision succeed and are more willing to put forth the efforts needed to implement and make the decision successful.

DELEGATING

I not only use all the brains I have, but all I can borrow.

–Woodrow Wilson

A good leader possesses the skills for effective delegation. It not only reduces the workload and stress of the leader but encourages employees to grow professionally, feel recognized, valued and trusted. The leader should not feel he/she is making others do his/her work. He/she should feel psychologically safe enough to take advantage of the strengths of the staff. The leader should try to know each member of staff well and use that knowledge when assigning tasks. It ensures that the right person is matched with the task that needs to be done. The effectiveness of the reference leader would be enhanced if he/she knows when to intervene directly and when to step back and allow others to provide input and directions. The leader should be willing to share power and control and promote leadership to flourish throughout the department. The following guideline may enhance delegating for results and employee development:

1. Delegate a specific task to a specific employee
2. Match assignments with the right employee with the needed abilities
3. Spell out assignment clearly (but leave room in the task description for ingenuity and initiative)
4. Give employees the authority needed for the responsibilities assigned to them
5. Create a safe, supportive and non-threatening atmosphere
6. Maintain an open communication channel between you and the employee
7. Remember that there is more than one way to get a task done
8. Provide employees with the needed resources--human and material–to complete the task
9. Evaluate employee execution of the delegated assignment
10. Acknowledge and reward a task well done.

COMMUNICATING

Communication could be defined as the many ways information is shared and/or exchanged between individuals or within a group of individuals. It could be seen as the lifeblood of any organization/department. It is what connects individuals, departments, and the whole organization. Daniel Katz and Robert Kahn call communication "the essence of organizations."[24] It is through good communication that a positive work environment is created and sustained, that decisions are made and implemented, and predetermined goals are attained. Effective communication skills are an important asset. The reference department leader should understand the process of communication and develop and refine the skills involved in effective communication.

The leader sets the tone of communications. The reference department leader would find the following guidelines useful. He/she should remember to:

- *Actively* listen to his/her staff
- Be mindful that messages are sent out both verbally and non-verbally
- Watch signals emitted so that the intended message is sent and received
- Watch his/her paraverbals
- Focus on the behavior and not on the employee
- Use good communication skills and concepts such as paraphrasing, mirroring, and reflective questioning
- Promote communication channels that flow in all directions–upward, downward, horizontal and diagonally
- Check for and remove barriers to effective communication
- Model effective communication
- Provide opportunities for communication
- Integrate grapevine and formal communication
- Evaluate the communication effectiveness of the reference department.

Effective communication could be enhanced when the leader:

1. Meets with his/her staff regularly
2. Asks them how they feel about their jobs
3. Has informal discussions with each member of his/her staff
4. Does not ask employees questions to which he/she is not prepared to receive honest responses
5. Views negative feedback as evidence of room for growth
6. Gives timely feedback
7. Encourages two-way interaction

8. Develops and uses active listening skills
9. Uses silence effectively.

STAFFING

Effective hiring is the first step to having a staff that will enable a unit to accomplish its goals. The reference leader should be skilled in the art and science of recruiting staff members. Some tips for hiring the best staff for the job include:

1. Do not be in a rush to hire
2. Search for people who are good fit for the job you need to do
3. Search for people who would fit into the team
4. Design and implement employment policies and procedures that foster thorough search and selection activities
5. Search until you locate the person who is right and not just "good enough" for the job
6. When a staff member leaves or when a new position is created, review the job description of the position and the ideal candidate for the job. Then design a job advertisement that targets the needed qualities.

Staff development is another crucial concept in adequate staffing of the reference department. It keeps staff knowledge and skills up-to-date and recharges their enthusiasm for their job. The initial training given to employees is not enough to help them perform well on their job. Very few skills and knowledge are acquired through the process of osmosis. The leader should ensure that there is a program in place to offer employees ongoing staff development opportunities. The program should address the identified needed skills and knowledge, and should conform to the current goals and to the future direction of the department. The cost for the ongoing staff development program could be kept low by organizing in-house training sessions and by inviting colleagues who possess the desired competencies to lead or to facilitate training sessions.

Gini is of the opinion that leaders should be committed to the belief that their success is directly connected to the success of their followers.[25] As much as possible the leader should have both the vertical and horizontal knowledge of how to get the job done. He/she should make a conscious effort to continuously learn and acquire new skills to enhance progressively high quality reference services. He/she must be able to learn, do and teach. All employees should also be encouraged to develop the culture of learning ad infinitum.

CONCLUSION

Leadership is difficult to explain and is a challenge to demonstrate. The role of the reference department leader is to get result–to adequately provide answers to patron reference questions. This can only be achieved through building and maintaining a winning team. The challenge that faces the reference department is to locate the person who can provide the leadership that would foster a winning reference department staff that will deliver quality reference services to patrons. There is no magic wand to produce the type of reference department that is responsive to the challenges of the 21st century. The quality, abilities and character of the reference leader are crucial. If he/she is to inspire and influence the staff to be effective he/she must acquire, develop and refine the competencies that are indispensable to leading the reference department of the 21st century. Nine competencies have been identified, defined, and discussed in this article. Leading has always been a complex responsibility and the only sure way to lead successfully is to exhibit the leadership behaviors that have the potential to promote result.

REFERENCES

1. Nozero, Victoria A. and Vaughan, Jason. (2000). "Utilization of Process Improvement to Manage Change in an Academic Library." *The Journal of Academic Librarianship* 26(6): p. 416.

2. Beckhard, Richard. "On Future Leaders." 1996 in *The Leader of the Future: New Visions, Strategies, and Practices for the Next Era.* [edited by] Frances Hesselbein, Marshall Goldsmith, Richard Beckhard. San Francisco: Jossey-Bass: p. 126.

3. "Leadership Excellence." (2001). *BLM National Training Center.* Retrieved on August 25, 2001 from World Wide Web http://www.ntc.blm.gov/leadership/leader_overview.html p. 1.

4. "Leadership vs. Management." (2001). The Public Service Leadership Network Retrieved on July 20, 2001 from World Wide Web: http://www.pslnet.org/LvsMGT.htm p. 1.

5. "Core Competencies for School Principals." (1995). The Education Review Office, Number 6, Winter 1995. Retrieved on July 30, 2001 from World Wide Web: http://www.ero.govt.nz/Publications/eers1995/95no6hl.htm#part3 p. 1.

6. Moore, Audrey D. (1996). "It Was the Best of Times, It Was . . . " *The Reference Librarian.* 54: p. 3.

7. Sherrer Johannah. (1996). "Thriving in Changing Times: Competencies for To-day's Reference Librarians." *The Reference Librarian.* 54: p. 11.

8. Northoude, Peter Guy. (1996). *Leadership: Theory and Practice.* Thousand Oaks, Sage Publications International Educational and Professional Publisher, p. 239.

9. Lunenburg, Fred and Allen C. Ornstein. (1990). *Educational Administration: Concepts and Practices.* Belmont CA: Wadsworth Publishing Company, p. 120.

10. Hesselbein, Frances. "The 'How to Be' Leader" in *The Leader of the Future: New Visions, Strategies, and Practices for the Next Era.* [edited by] Frances Hesselbein, Marshall Goldsmith, Richard Beckhard. San Francisco: Jossey-Bass: p. 122

11. Harris, Jim. (1995). *Getting Employees to Fall in Love with Your Company.* New York: American Management Association, p. 20.

12. Senge, Pleter M. (1993). *The Fifth Discipline: The Art and Practice of the Learning Organization.* New York: Doubleday/Currency: p. 9.

13. Sullivan, Jeremiah J. 1992. "Japanese Management Philosophies: From the Vacuous to the Brilliant." *California Management Review, Berkeley;* 1992 (winter) 34: (2): p. 80-81.

14. Advancing Employee Productivity. "Motivation: Self-fulfilling Prophecy The Pygmalion Effect at Work." Retrieved on September 12, 2001 from World Wide Web http://www.accel-team.com/pygmalion/prophecy_01.html p. 1.

15. Goble, David S. 1997. " Managing in a Change Environment: From Coping to Comfort." *Library Administration & Management* 11: p. 151-56.

16. "The X Y and Z of Management Theory." Retrieved on August 30, 2001 from World Wide Web http://www.comp.glam.ac.uk/teaching/ismanagement/manstyles-t4.htm p. 2.

17. Ibid p. 2.

18. Lunenburg, Fred and Allen C. Ornstein. (1990). *Educational Administration: Concepts and Practices.* Belmont CA: Wadsworth Publishing Company: p. 133-34.

19. Ibid p. 133.

20. Alan H. Anderson and Anna Kyprianou. *Effective Organizational Behaviour: A Skills and Activity-based Approach.* Cambridge, Mass.: Blackwell Publishers, 1994, p. 66-67.

21. Riggs, Donald E. and Vivian M. Sykes. (1993). "The Time for Transformational Leadership Is Now." *Journal of Library Administration* 18: p. 55-68.

22. Dusky, Kathy L. 2001 "Library Leadership in Times of Change." *PNLA Quarterly* 65:(2): p. 16.

23. "Twenty-First Century Leadership." Retrieved on August 30, 2001 from World Wide Web http://www.dashhouse.com/Sermons/2001/SALT/010129.htm p. 1.

24. Katz, Daniel and Robert L. Kahn. (1978). *The Social Psychology of Organizations,* 2nd ed. New York: Wiley: p. 223.

25. Gini, Al. "Leadership: Keys of an Effective Leader." Retrieved on August 30, 2001 from World Wide Web http://www.tsbj.com/editorial/03010714.htm p. 1.

Training the New Head of Reference: Focusing on the Supervising Relationship as Technique

Philip C. Howze

SUMMARY. A predictable shortage of librarians in public and academic libraries, due to the progressive retirement of the baby boomers and the lure of lucrative positions in the private sector, signifies the need for libraries to change the way heads of reference are hired and retained. Years of previous supervisory experience as a job requirement will need to be replaced with agreement to participate in a positive and substantive training regimen for new supervisors. This article looks at why supervisors need training, assessing the competencies of a new supervisor, applied training for the new head of reference, and consequences of failing to train new supervisors. Examples of techniques for establishing the training milieu are suggested. *[Article copies available for a fee from The Haworth Document Delivery Service: 1-800-HAWORTH. E-mail address: <docdelivery@haworthpress.com> Website: <http://www.HaworthPress.com> © 2003 by The Haworth Press, Inc. All rights reserved.]*

KEYWORDS. Heads of reference, supervisors, managers, supervisor training programs, public services, reference departments

Philip C. Howze, MLS, MPA, is Social Sciences Librarian, Morris Library, Southern Illinois University at Carbondale, Mailcode 6632, Carbondale, IL 62901-6632 (E-mail: phowze@lib.siu.edu).

[Haworth co-indexing entry note]: "Training the New Head of Reference: Focusing on the Supervising Relationship as Technique." Howze, Philip C. Co-published simultaneously in *The Reference Librarian* (The Haworth Information Press, an imprint of The Haworth Press, Inc.) No. 81, 2003, pp. 51-58; and: *Managing the Twenty-First Century Reference Department: Challenges and Prospects* (ed: Kwasi Sarkodie-Mensah) The Haworth Information Press, an imprint of The Haworth Press, Inc., 2003, pp. 51-58. Single or multiple copies of this article are available for a fee from The Haworth Document Delivery Service [1-800-HAWORTH, 9:00 a.m. - 5:00 p.m. (EST). E-mail address: docdelivery@haworthpress.com].

There will soon be a profound shortage of librarians in public and academic libraries, due to the progressive retirement of the baby boomer generation and the lure of lucrative positions for librarians in the private sector. One of the effects of such a shortage is that there will be even fewer applicants for reference manager positions than ever. Libraries will need to change the way they hire and cultivate heads of reference, in order to sustain leadership in this vital functional unit within public services. One such change will involve moving from "previous supervisory experience" as a job requirement, to "participation in a positive and substantive training regimen for new supervisors."

There are many experienced, talented librarians who may be willing to direct reference departments if assurances were made that the experience would not be similar to being thrown into the proverbial lion's den; and that practical training and ongoing support would be available as needed. The purpose of this article is to aid in the recruitment of new heads of reference by articulating the need for supervisor training for experienced librarians lacking supervisory experience.

WHY SUPERVISORS NEED TRAINING

New heads of reference, whether they have previous supervisory experience or not, need training. In order to function effectively in a new environment, or in a new role within the same environment, a person needs to know the local policies, procedures and routines of the inhabitants. Additionally, the training milieu allows both the supervisor trainee and the persons being supervised to practice agreeing on the goals of supervision and performance.

The head of reference who is hired externally has a lot to learn about the environment into which she or he has entered. Few supervisors can function effectively without knowing the local policies, procedures and routines, or "the way things are done." The "way" generally means a series, if not a matrix, of routines.

There are two types of routines, formal and informal. Experience teaches that informal routines can be as powerful as the formal ones, because over time, a practice becomes a rule. Formal routines, most often, are functions of time. Examples include reference desk scheduling (some practitioners have a distinct preference for certain times of the day); lunch times and break times; and regularly scheduled meetings. Informal routines are usually related to habit, custom, or worker accommodation. Examples include such matters as bringing good things to eat, celebrating birthdays, employee recognition events, retirements and holidays. The new head of reference needs to know these things, and morale problems can ensue if the person does not know or value long-established customs.

Seniority, whether real (formal, written policy exists) or implied (informal, no policy exists) is a prime example of a routine that can cause major issues if the custom is not followed. Also, the internally hired (or promoted) head has to "learn" to adjust his or her reading of local policies and procedures from that of compliance to ensuring compliance by others.

One of the most unsettling experiences for a new supervising librarian, particularly if he or she is the sensitive type, is post-honeymoon loneliness. To ward off the feelings of abandonment, reference heads, particularly the ones who were hired internally, try to sustain old friendships as if nothing were different in their lives. Sometimes, it even works. More often than not, however, the relationships have changed– because the person has changed positions, from co-worker to supervisor. Supervisor training can facilitate the transition from fellow librarian to head of reference. Supervisor training for head librarians could result in a decrease in service failures or complaints, as well as in professional differences of opinion.

An open training milieu, the environment in which both the new supervisor and those newly supervised share in the orientation, allows both the supervisor-in-training and the persons being supervised to practice agreeing on the goals of supervision and performance. This actually occurs quite naturally, for a while. During the first two weeks on the job, most people will forgive just about anything, which is probably why the employment phase is termed the "honeymoon" period. Few libraries take maximum advantage of it, however; what tends to happen is the new head of reference is scheduled for a series of meetings and appointments ranging from human resources to campus-wide orientations for new employees, commonly held outside of the library. The open training milieu must be planned, organized, and well coordinated, in order to set the culture of collegiality from the new head's first day on the job.

ASSESSING THE COMPETENCIES OF A SUPERVISOR

The head of reference is not an assembly line supervisor. Supervising the work of highly educated people requires peer status, membership in a common profession, and librarianship is only one example. Effective training, including supervisor training, should be tailored to the learning style of the trainee and the specific work setting. Still, there are general training principles that apply to most people, regardless of learning style or place, because they are tied to learning facility and self-esteem. Research in the area of training supervising therapists (Getz, 1999) has identified a process to assess the competencies of the supervisor that may have applicability to the reference manager, as practicing librarian.

Assessing the competencies of the supervisor, as a technique, can contribute positively to the open training environment, if done carefully and with the intent of building on pre-existing strengths. Who conducts the assessment? For the head of reference, whoever supervises the position (associate dean or director of public services), or the staff development and training librarian (if the library has one), can assess the competencies of the person. After pre-existing competencies have been assessed, the actual training, or what one needs to know in order to be an effective head of reference, begins.

TRAINING AS TECHNIQUE

A number of managers believe they could save on training expenses if the right people were hired in the first place. Everybody needs some training, including supervisors. There are as many training techniques available as there are training consultants. Brown (1999) recommends three steps to effective training: (1) The training relationship begins with the job description; (2) begin the training with a routine of activities, because supervisors especially need routine activities in order to acquire the ability to train and supervise others; and (3) the purpose for the training must be clear.

In addition to providing a routine of activities for the new library supervisor to do, the person should be provided with learning opportunities that are not so routine, including tutorials and clerkships in such areas as library budgeting, personnel and systems. Cross-training in other areas of management is an effective way of maintaining productivity levels when a workforce is shrinking (Hankins and Kleiner, 1995). Broadwell (1993) notes, as a professional trainer of supervisors, that any "technique" that has the greatest chance of working is one based on the management style of the organization, because top management decides which behaviors get rewarded and which get punished in the organization. Libraries are no exception.

USE OF SELF-DISCLOSURE

The supervisory milieu requires highly active participation on the part of the supervisor trainee. Besides learning routine tasks, the new supervisor will need to learn the techniques of supervising other professionals. One such technique is the use of self-disclosure, also found in the literature on supervising therapists (Ladany and Lehrman-Waterman, 1999). In general, self-disclosures have been defined as personal statements made about oneself to another (Watkins, 1990). According to Friedlander and Ward (1984), a supervisor can lean toward one of three interrelated styles: attractive (characterized by friendliness, warmth, and flexibility), interpersonally sensitive (characterized as invested, therapeutic, and intuitive), or task-oriented (characterized by goal orientation, pragmatism, and structure). Whether or not a supervisor self-discloses would be a function of the supervisory styles in which he or she engages. In the relationship between the reference manager as trainee and librarians, the judicious use of self-disclosure that is non-condescending could be very helpful, particularly when interacting with librarians new to the practice of reference. This supervisory technique is recommended as part of the training the new head of reference receives.

ADDITIONAL ISSUES RELATED TO TRAINING

Workforce demographics are changing, and organizations, including libraries, must figure out how to respond to those changes. Matthews (1998) notes, "Organizations must [also] address how to successfully manage employees with diverse lifestyles, single parents, unmarrieds (sic) with spousal equivalents, gay couples, job-sharers, two-income families or physically challenged individuals." For the new head of reference, training can be a period in which these matters and others may be addressed, including cultural diversity, intellectual freedom, and workplace accommodation for the disabled.

THE SUPERVISORY WORKING ALLIANCE

One of the benefits of an open supervisory milieu is the opportunity to develop a positive supervisory alliance. The "supervisory working alliance" (Bordin, 1983) consists of three interrelated variables: agreement on the goals of supervision, agreement on the tasks of supervision, and an emotional bond between the trainee and the supervisor. In academic libraries, these variables are particularly germane to supervising a library unit.

Agreement on the goals of supervision (strengthening question negotiation skills, for example) can do much to defuse a power dynamic in the supervisor-worker relationship, and promote mutuality of goal attainment. Agreement on the tasks of supervision (observing an experienced practitioner at the reference desk, for example) can promote the sharing of information without judgement, instead of one party capitulating to the teacher-student dynamic often at work when reference librarians train each other. The mutuality that stems from agreement on the tasks of supervision leads to an increased likelihood of a professional exchange instead of a parental one.

The presence of an emotional bond (trust, liking and caring) will likely facilitate the first two agreements. It is much easier for people who trust each other to work together than those who do not. In libraries, the presence of such a bond is often based on longevity and shared experiences, especially if the reference manager came up "through the ranks" with some of those librarians he or she now supervises. Liking is not the imperative, however; trusting the reference manager is far more enduring as a positive outcome of the supervisory working alliance, even in the absence of close personal friendships.

CONSEQUENCES OF FAILING TO TRAIN

A number of libraries do not see the need to provide formal training for their supervisors and managers. The notion that hiring the most qualified applicant for the head of reference position will "transport" quality into the local institution, without training, is a mistaken one. It is not uncommon for library administrators to find themselves concluding, sooner than they had hoped, that they have not hired the reference manager of their desires. Merit (1998) notes,

> If that's the way you pick your supervisors, and if that's the way you drop them out there to sink or swim, without providing training or leadership, then you should not be surprised if this is the kind of department you get: No cooperation among the staff. Grumbling about the way the work comes to them from the previous department, but not caring how it gets passed on to the next group. And on and on it goes.

Strategic intervention, including training and support, can prevent situations such as this.

CONCLUSION

Libraries will need to change the way they hire and retain heads of reference, in order to sustain leadership in this vital functional unit within public services. One such change will involve moving from "previous supervisory experience" as a job requirement, to "participation in a positive and substantive training regimen for new supervisors." New heads of reference need training. In an open training environment both the new supervisor and the newly supervised share in the orientation and practice agreeing on the goals of supervision and performance. Assessment of competencies can be an effective tool if used to build on pre-existing strengths. When it comes to what kind of training, any technique that has the greatest chance of working is one based on the management style of the organization, but the open training milieu can be successfully employed in libraries. The judicious use of self-disclosure, once learned by the new head of reference, as technique, can be helpful when interacting with and training new librarians. Of highest importance, however, is the cultivation of an effective supervisory working alliance, based on trust and peer regard. A working alliance is based on shared learning, which will be key as libraries search for new leaders.

REFERENCES

Bordin, E.S. (1983). "A Working Alliance Based Model of Supervision," *The Counseling Psychologist* 1 (I), 35-41.

Broadwell, Martin M. (1993). "How to Train Experienced Supervisors," *Training* 30 (May), 61-66.

Brown, Stephen. (1999). "Failing to Train and Coach New Hires is Failing to Manage," *Supervision* 60 (March), 18-19.

Friedlander, M.L. and L.G. Ward (1984). "Development and Validation of the Supervisory Styles Inventory," *Journal of Counseling Psychology* 36, 149-157.

Getz, Hildy G. (1999). "Assessment of Clinical Supervisor Competencies," *Journal of Counseling & Development* 77 (Fall), 491-497.

Hankins, Christine and Brian H. Kleiner. (1995). "New Developments in Supervisor Training," *Industrial & Commercial Training* 27 (1), 26-32.

Ladany, Nicholas and Deborah E. Lehrman-Waterman. (1999). "The Content and Frequency of Supervisor Self-disclosures and Their Relationship to Supervisor Style and the Supervisory Working Alliance," *Counselor Education & Supervision* 38 (March), 143-160.

Matthews, Audrey. (1998). "Diversity: A Principle of Human Resource Management," *Public Personnel Management* 27 (Summer), 175-185.

Merit, Don. (1998). "Don't Pick a Bad Supervisor," *American Printer* 221 (May), 78.

Watkins, C.E., Jr. (1990). The Effects of Counselor Self-disclosure: A Research Review," *The Counseling Psychologist* 18, 477-500.

SUGGESTED READING

Giesecke, Joan, ed. (1997). *Practical Help for New Supervisors, 3rd Edition*, Chicago IL, ALA Editions.

Collaborative Leadership:
A Model for Reference Services

Kathryn M. Crowe

SUMMARY. In 1991, Joseph C. Rost published *Leadership for the 21st Century* (Praeger) in which he presented a definition of leadership that focused on the influence relationship among leaders and followers rather than on the traits of the leader or the functions of leadership. Rost's model is useful for academic reference leaders who usually head a group of professionals who are involved in a variety of responsibilities that require them to be leaders. This article applies Rost's theories to academic reference leadership and explores a model that will provide for better job satisfaction for librarians and improved services to library users. *[Article copies available for a fee from The Haworth Document Delivery Service: 1-800-HAWORTH. E-mail address: <docdelivery@haworthpress.com> Website: <http://www.HaworthPress.com> © 2003 by The Haworth Press, Inc. All rights reserved.]*

KEYWORDS. Reference services, leadership, academic libraries

INTRODUCTION

It is redundant, of course, to state that academic libraries have changed over the last fifteen years. They have transformed from build-

Kathryn M. Crowe is Head, Reference Department, Jackson Library, PO Box 26175, Greensboro, NC 27402-6175 (E-mail: kathy_crowe@uncg.edu).

[Haworth co-indexing entry note]: "Collaborative Leadership: A Model for Reference Services." Crowe, Kathryn M. Co-published simultaneously in *The Reference Librarian* (The Haworth Information Press, an imprint of The Haworth Press, Inc.) No. 81, 2003, pp. 59-69; and: *Managing the Twenty-First Century Reference Department: Challenges and Prospects* (ed: Kwasi Sarkodie-Mensah) The Haworth Information Press, an imprint of The Haworth Press, Inc., 2003, pp. 59-69. Single or multiple copies of this article are available for a fee from The Haworth Document Delivery Service [1-800-HAWORTH, 9:00 a.m. - 5:00 p.m. (EST). E-mail address: docdelivery@haworthpress.com].

ings with collections of materials to dynamic organizations that provide access to vast resources. Academic reference departments and the nature of reference work have been impacted significantly by this transformation. While WHAT reference librarians do is not so different–we still assist users in finding and evaluating information, provide instruction in using resources, and select materials–HOW we do it, however, and the tools and resources we use have changed dramatically. Reference departments have responded to these changes by providing new services and restructuring their organizations to be more efficient. Libraries have experimented with tiered reference service, using paraprofessionals at service desks to allow professional librarians time for other responsibilities and implementing team structures to provide public service. With new technologies available, reference service has expanded to include such innovations as e-mail reference, online tutorials and user guides, and real-time digital reference service. The issue of leadership for academic reference departments in this age of transformation, however, has not been carefully examined. While there have been numerous articles about the *types* of leaders needed for academic libraries and the *functions* that these leaders should perform, the actual *process* of leading an academic reference department has not been adequately explored.

COLLABORATIVE LEADERSHIP FOR TRANSFORMATION

The issue of the leadership process is not unique to librarianship but has also been a controversy in leadership studies. In his 1978 landmark study, *Leadership*, James MacGregor Burns lamented:

> If we know all too much about our leaders, we know far too little about leadership. We fail to grasp the essence of leadership that is relevant to the modern age and hence we cannot agree even on the standards by which to measure, recruit, and reject it. Is leadership simply innovation–cultural or political? Is it essentially inspiration? Mobilization of followers? Goal setting? Goal fulfillment? Is a leader the definer of values? Satisfier of needs? If leaders require followers, who lead whom from where to where, and why? How do leaders lead followers without being wholly led by followers? Leadership is one of the most observed and least understood phenomena on earth.[1]

Burns was further frustrated that neither had a school of leadership been developed nor had there been literature that combined theories of leadership and followership. Burns identified two basic types of leadership–transactional and transforming. He defined transactional leadership as the relationship between most leaders and followers whereby leaders approach followers with the purpose of exchanging one thing for another, such as jobs for votes. On the other hand, according to Burns, transforming leadership seeks to engage followers more completely and can potentially turn followers into leaders.[2]

While Burns' book is a classic text, he still did not provide a cogent definition of leadership. In 1991, Joseph C. Rost published *Leadership for the Twenty First Century*, in which he attempted to provide a definition for leadership in the post-industrial age. Rost built on Burns' theory of transforming leadership. He was highly critical of leadership scholarship and claimed that no plausible definition had been provided. He further asserted that leadership studies had focused entirely too much on leadership traits, personality characteristics, goals, and management of organizations. According to Rost, leadership studies had been more interested in content rather than the actual process of leadership.[3] He contended that scholars and practitioners emphasized leadership's peripheral elements and content instead of the "essential nature of leadership as a relationship."[4]

After a thorough analysis of leadership scholarship from the early part of the 20th century through the 1980s, Rost offered a definition of leadership for the post-industrial world: "Leadership is an influence relationship among leaders and followers who intend real changes that reflect their mutual purposes."[5] Rost thus emphasized the *relationship* between leaders and followers as opposed to focusing only on the leader and his/her traits. "Leadership is not what the leader does but what the leaders and collaborators do together to change organizations."[6] He further embellished his definition by explaining that the influence relationship is multidirectional and noncoercive. Both leaders and followers must intend changes and these changes must be substantive and transforming. According to Rost, leaders and followers develop mutual purposes rather than goals.[7] He further recommended that organizations effect change by:

1. Deciding on the proposed change.
2. Leaders and followers influencing others in the organization to support the change.

3. Planning the change by leaders and followers developing an outline that reflects their mutual purposes.
4. Gathering and analyzing information and deciding on the direction.
5. Building the agenda.[8]

While Rost emphasized the importance of noncoercive influence between leaders and followers and the need for followers to be an active part of the leadership process, he still realized that it is an unequal relationship. Leaders usually have more influence because "they are willing to commit more of the power resources they possess to the relationship and they are more skilled at putting those power resources to work to influence others in the relationship."[9] At the same time, there are times when followers may exert more influence than leaders and will take initiative to accomplish certain purposes. Thus, followers can become leaders and are active in the leadership relationship rather than passive recipients of the leader's influence.[10]

TRANSFORMATION OF REFERENCE SERVICES

Over the past decade, the needs of academic library users have altered considerably. Because students and faculty can access catalogs, databases, and full-text resources remotely, traffic at the traditional reference desk has dropped dramatically. At the same time, the demand for instruction and training has risen because users need much guidance in using these electronic resources effectively.[11] Changes in higher education have affected libraries as well. Distance learning initiatives and returning adult students require new library services such as 24/7 off-campus access to resources, off-campus training, direct document delivery and remote assistance in using resources.

Reference leaders have explored numerous methods to restructure reference service to respond to these changing needs. One of the first reports was Virginia Massey-Burzio's 1992 article that described the tiered reference service at Brandeis University. Brandeis established an information desk that was staffed by graduate students to handle routine directional questions while in-depth research inquiries were handled by appointments with reference librarians. Massey-Burzio argued that most questions received at the reference desk were very routine and professional librarians' time and expertise was much better spent focusing on specialized research.[12] Numerous other articles appeared throughout the 1990s that recommended tiered reference service, using paraprofessionals at the reference desk, sending librarians out to academic departments, floating reference librarians, cooperative reference, and developing expert systems to handle routine questions.[13]

These models of restructuring reference were consistent with trends in academic libraries in the 1990s. Many libraries experimented with new structures both to provide better customer service and also to offer new opportunities for librarians and staff.[14] In particular, Richard Sweeney in his 1994 article, "Leadership in the Post-Hierarchical Library," called for a complete reengineering of the library that focused on customer satisfaction. Sweeney recommended cross functional, networked teams which would require excellent communication and result in distributed decision-making and better accountability.[15] The team structure was implemented in many libraries including the University of Arizona. There, librarians focused on meeting the needs of users by examining the mission of the library, critically examining the value of their work activities, and making productive changes. Staff from many units of the library participated in public service teams and discovered new skills and qualities they did not know they had.[16]

Since the late 1990s, the increased use of the Web as an information source and as a platform for service has created further implications for reference services. Students rely on the Web for much of their research and it is a new challenge for librarians to guide students to reliable resources. Some reference librarians feel very threatened by the dwindling numbers of reference questions and are concerned that they will be replaced by search engines and commercial enterprises.[17] Librarians have responded by utilizing current technology to adapt their services to contemporary needs. New developments such as online tutorials, online reference, subject portals, online user guides and personalized library interfaces have been implemented in many academic libraries. Reference departments, however, usually continue to be structured in a traditional manner and around a specific place. In a 2000 *College and Research Libraries* article, Chris Ferguson provided a comprehensive model for reference services in the 21st century. Ferguson urged librarians to envision desirable services and then determine what structures and support services are necessary to support these services.[18] He recommended a combination of on-site and off-site services ranging from online user aids and chat reference service to appointments with subject specialists.[19] To implement such a tiered service, librarians must explore new roles and functions and collaborate across administrative lines both within and without the library. The role of the reference leader, according to Ferguson, is to bring people and resources together to facilitate change in innovative and productive ways.[20]

REFERENCE LEADERSHIP FOR TRANSFORMATION

With all the myriad discussions on how to restructure reference services, there has been very little work on reference leadership or management during this age of transformation. One article by Maureen Sullivan explored extensively the middle-management role in libraries and identified elements similar to Rost. She noted that as support staff perform more computer work, library managers have less direct knowledge of the work they supervise and rely on staff to solve their own problems. Because of this trend, the manager's role has shifted away from "one of direction and control to one of guidance and coordination, the role of staff shifts from that of subordinate to a partner or participant in the accomplishment of work and the achievement of organizational goals."[21] Sullivan recommended that library middle managers establish working relationships based on trust and mutual respect, allow themselves to be influenced as well as exercise influence and share power by creating meaningful opportunities for staff involvement in problem solving, decision making, and planning.[22]

Barbara Dewey provided one of the few analyses of leadership among those who are usually thought of as "followers" in libraries. She examined the leadership qualities needed by front-line public service librarians, especially entry or mid-level librarians. She suggested that they must be adept managers of programs, services, and activities and provide leadership in evaluating library services, designing library instruction programs and managing specific projects.[23]

Only one article in recent years addressed leadership and the head of reference position specifically. In 1994, Nofsinger and Bosch outlined the specific roles of this position and identified necessary people-management functions such as training and coordination, socialization and the corporate culture, supervision and daily operations, communication, and performance evaluation. They also stressed the role of technology facilitator.[24] They primarily focused on these specific functions and did not address leadership except to note:

> As a front line manager, the head of reference accomplishes work through team leadership of colleagues and other staff in a climate of trust and respect. Frequently the reference manager leads by

pulling rather than pushing, inspires rather than orders, jointly sets expectations for service and then works side-by-side with colleagues to accomplish them, and empowers others to use their own initiative and unique abilities.[25]

THE COLLABORATIVE MODEL FOR REFERENCE LEADERS

Rost's theory of transforming leadership has useful applications for academic reference departments. Like their teaching faculty colleagues, reference librarians are often very independent and creative thinkers. Collaborative leadership can take advantage of such minds and result in better services and programs for users as well as increased job satisfaction for all members of the unit. In addition to public service, reference librarians usually have numerous other responsibilities such as library instruction, subject liaisons or bibliographers, campus faculty obligations, and professional service. They often assume leadership roles in the department or library such as supervision of graduate students, library instruction coordination or collection management. Younger librarians who may be more technologically savvy usually take on leadership in that area by serving as webmasters and developing online aids. Many of these responsibilities, especially those that reach outside the library, take place away from the direct supervision of the department head. Because these activities can foster needed library services as well as professional growth, they need to be encouraged and supported by the reference head. Ideas for new services and programs should come from all members of the unit. Team members should accept the leadership role for these projects; the team leader can assume the follower role and, at the same time, provide overall support. This cooperation creates an atmosphere that shares knowledge, encourages creativity and results in better service for library users. In addition, collaborative leadership provides more opportunity for job enrichment and professional development.

A useful example of collaborative leadership was the trial of chat reference service implemented at the University of North Carolina at Greensboro in Spring 2001. This trial followed Rost's process of collaborative leadership described earlier. The reference department decided to explore this new service (proposed change). The most qualified person to lead the effort was the newest librarian in the department who had the most technical knowledge (leaders and followers influencing others). She researched software, set up the trial, trained others to use the software, recruited assistance from the technology unit, and scheduled librarians to cover the service (planning the change). After the trial was completed, the department discussed the trial and its strengths and weaknesses (gathering and analyzing information). With some changes, we decided to continue the service the following fall (building the agenda).

This project was truly a collaborative effort with a librarian from the team providing leadership while others in the unit, including the department head, assumed the role of followers. Because we were one unit, in a larger organization, it was the responsibility of the department head to ensure that this project was a priority and to work with library administration and other library units to gain support for software, equipment and other resources. By bringing together the talents and knowledge of several people, a successful project was designed and implemented and a new service was developed.

While Rost's model provides a useful framework for the leadership process, there are flaws. Although Rost rejected identifying specific traits for leaders, there are certain abilities that successful library leaders (or any leader) must have. In this time of major change in academic libraries, it is especially imperative that leaders be able to embrace innovation and experiment with new opportunities. Indeed, Rebecca Martin in her article "Library Leaders for the 21st Century" stated that managing change and viewing change as an opportunity will likely be the most critical criteria for academic library leaders.[26] Sweeney recommended leaders that are strategists with a vision and the will to achieve it. He also argued that leaders must also be superb communicators who listen, speak, and write well and are creative and encourage creativity in others. In addition, leaders must be risk-takers.[27] A January 2001 *Library Issues Briefings for Faculty and Administrators* stated that library leaders will require "an extraordinary ability to maintain a delicate and continually shifting balance in the management of technical, financial, and human resources to serve the academic mission of our colleges and universities."[28]

These traits and functions can be applied more specifically to reference leaders. Reference heads must have a thorough knowledge of traditional and current reference practices and be able to balance between them. As mentioned above, they must be risk-takers in order to move reference services forward into the 21st century. Reference leaders need to develop a vision for their unit and articulate that vision within the unit and to the library and campus. It is well established that excellent communication skills are essential for any leader. As middle managers, reference heads must be able to communicate well with his/her team and also collaborate effectively with other units and library administration. In other words, they need to communicate up, down, and across! As supervisors, reference leaders also need to be effective motivators and serve as mentors to new librarians.

Training for leadership in libraries is obviously a major issue and one that probably deserves an entire article of its own. MLS programs do not usually provide enough management or leadership education so librarians need to take advantage of other opportunities such as business school classes, workshops, professional seminars, and other types of continuing education in order to gain leadership and communication skills. Academic libraries need to provide opportunities for staff to take advantage of leadership education. Developing current and future leaders will ensure strong libraries for the 21st century.

CONCLUSION

In this age of transformation in libraries, reference departments are responding to many changes in information needs. They are offering new programs and developing new methods to provide traditional services. To facilitate these changes reference units need to examine their organizational structure and leadership processes. Rost's collaborative model can serve as a useful paradigm for the leadership process. His definition of leadership, which focused on the relationships involved rather than specific characteristics, seems especially applicable in the 21st century. In order to provide the complex variety of services needed for higher education, reference departments need librarians with many types of knowledge and skills who should provide leadership when a project falls into their area of expertise. Such collaboration within a unit or team encourages creative thinking and increased productivity. Furthermore, reference departments need to work across units in order to provide excellent services. Work teams are often created where the leader is not a direct supervisor. Here, the influence relationship becomes particularly emphasized. Collaborative leadership, then, is a model that can create a positive and productive working environment that serves both employees and customers well.

REFERENCES

1. James MacGregor Burns, *Leadership* (New York: Harper & Row, 1978), 1-2.

2. Ibid., 3-4.

3. Joseph C. Rost, *Leadership in the Twenty-First Century* (Westport, CN: Praeger, 1992), 3-4.

4. Ibid., 5.

5. Ibid., 102.

6. Joseph C. Rost, "Leadership Development in the New Millennium," *The Journal of Leadership Studies* 1 (November 1993): 101.

7. Ibid., 102-103.

8. Joseph C. Rost and Anthony Smith, "Leadership: A Postindustrial Approach," *European Management Journal* 10 (June 1992), 196.

9. Rost, *Leadership in the 21st Century*, 112.

10. Ibid.

11. For example for the last two years at Jackson Library at UNCG, reference desk statistics have dropped approximately 15% while instruction statistics rose 4-6%.

12. Virginia Massey-Burzio, "Reference Encounters of a Different Kind: A Symposium," *Journal of Academic Librarianship* 18 (November 1992): 277-278.

13. See, for example: Karen Storin Summerhill. "The High Cost of Reference: The Need to Reassess Services and Service Delivery." *The Reference Librarian* 43 (1994): 71-85; Terry Ann Mood. "Of Sundials and Digital Watches: A Further Step Toward the New Paradigm of Reference." *Reference Services Review* 22 (Fall 1994): 27-32+; Jackie Mardikian and Martin Kesselman. "Beyond the Desk Enhanced Reference Staffing for the Electronic Library." *Reference Services Review* 23 (Spring 1995): 21-28+; Williams L. Whitson. "Differentiated Service: A New Reference Model." *Journal of Academic Librarianship* 21 (March 1995): 103-110.

14. See, for example: Susan Lee. "Organizational Change in Research Libraries." *Journal of Library Administration* 18 (1993): 129-143; Richard Sweeney. "Leadership in the Post-Hierarchical Library." *Library Trends* 43 (Summer 1994): 62-95; David W. Lewis. "Making Academic Reference Services Work." *College and Research Libraries* 55 (September 1994): 445-456; Terrence Mech. "Leadership and the Evolution of Academic Librarianship." *Journal of Academic Librarianship* 22 (September 1996): 345-353; Donald E. Riggs. "What's in Store for Academic Libraries? Leadership and Management Issues," *Journal of Academic Librarianship* 23 (January 1997): 3-8; Sion M. Honea. "Transforming Administration in Academic Libraries," *Journal of Academic Librarianship* 23 (May 1997): 183-191; Rebecca R. Martin. "Recruiting a Library Leader for the 21st Century." *Journal of Library Administration* 24 (1997): 47-58; Cheryl LaGuardia, ed. *Recreating the Academic Library: Breaking Virtual Ground.* New York: Neal-Schuman Publishers, Inc., (1998); Terrance F. Mech and Gerard B. McCabe, eds. *Leadership and Academic Librarians.* Westport, CN: Greenwood Press, 1998.

15. Sweeney, 74.

16. Janet S. Fore, R. Cecilia Knight, and Carrie Russell, "Leadership for User Services in the Academic Library," *Journal of Academic Librarianship* 19 (1993): 99-102.

17. Ann Grodzins Lipow, " 'In Your Face' Reference Service," *Library Journal* 124 (August 1999): 50.

18. Chris D. Ferguson. " 'Shaking the Conceptual Foundations,' Too: Integrating Research and Technology Support for the Next Generation of Information Service," *College and Research Libraries* 61 (July 2000): 302.

19. Ibid., 305.

20. Ibid., 308-309.

21. Maureen Sullivan, "The Changing Role of the Middle Manager in Research Libraries," *Library Trends* 41 (Fall 1992): 271-272.

22. Ibid., 278-279.

23. Barbara I. Dewey, "Public Services Librarians in the Academic Community: The Imperative for Leadership," in *Leadership and Academic Librarians*, eds. Terrence F. Mech and Gerard B. McCabe (Westport CN: Greenwood Press, 1998), 94.

24. Mary M. Nofsinger and Allan W. Bosch, "Roles of the Head of Reference: From the 1990s to the 21st Century," *The Reference Librarian* 42 (1994) 88-92.

25. Ibid., 95.

26. Martin, 46-47.

27. Sweeney, 85.

28. Terry Metz, "Wanted: Library Leaders for a Discontinuous Future." *Library Issues: Briefings for Faculty and Administrators*, 21 (January 2001): 2.

It Takes a Village to Manage
the 21st Century Reference Department

Paula McMillen
Loretta Rielly

SUMMARY. Reference services at Oregon State University's Valley Library have undergone several reorganizations in response to institutional changes, shifting service needs and patron demands. Part of this history includes training for and functioning in team-based management. We have now evolved to a management model that utilizes workgroups and an advisory and coordinating council to assist in running the department. We find this model provides flexibility, sharing of the workload and professional development opportunities, all of which are essential in today's tumultuous reference environment. We will describe the functioning, potential hazards and multiple advantages of this model. *[Article copies available for a fee from The Haworth Document Delivery Service: 1-800-HAWORTH. E-mail address: <docdelivery@haworthpress.com> Website: <http://www.HaworthPress.com> © 2003 by The Haworth Press, Inc. All rights reserved.]*

KEYWORDS. Management models, reference services, participatory management, professional development, team management

Paula McMillen is Social Science Reference Librarian, and Loretta Rielly is currently Humanities Librarian and formerly Head of Reference, Valley Library, Oregon State University, Corvallis, OR 97331 (E-mail: Paula.McMillen@orst.edu; Loretta.Rielly@orst.edu).

[Haworth co-indexing entry note]: "It Takes a Village to Manage the 21st Century Reference Department." McMillen, Paula, and Loretta Rielly. Co-published simultaneously in *The Reference Librarian* (The Haworth Information Press, an imprint of The Haworth Press, Inc.) No. 81, 2003, pp. 71-87; and: *Managing the Twenty-First Century Reference Department: Challenges and Prospects* (ed: Kwasi Sarkodie-Mensah) The Haworth Information Press, an imprint of The Haworth Press, Inc., 2003, pp. 71-87. Single or multiple copies of this article are available for a fee from The Haworth Document Delivery Service [1-800-HAWORTH, 9:00 a.m. - 5:00 p.m. (EST). E-mail address: docdelivery@haworthpress.com].

10.1300/J120v39n81_07

The reference services literature proclaims that change is THE major character in this unfolding drama with ambiguity playing a supporting role. David Lewis and others remark on the "radical changes" (Lewis, 1994, p. 445) generated by new technologies, mushrooming amounts and kinds of accessible information, shifting demographics and increasing size of our patron base, greater demands for traditional and new services, and static or declining budgets and staffs (Barnello, 1996; Nofsinger & Bosch, 1994; Papandrea, 1998). The reference department at Oregon State University is certainly not unique in its quest to merge new and traditional services and to accommodate the expanding needs of its local and distant users. However, after mergers and expansions of departments and programs, creation and dissolution of formal and informal teams, the destination we've reached is somewhat unique: a hybrid management model that addresses the complexity of our work.

We'll briefly describe the changing reference scene, some alternative models of reference service and our evolution to the current configuration. Finally we'll talk about our use of a Reference and Instruction Council that shares accountability and decision making. We'll discuss the advantages and potential problem areas for using such a model.

WHAT NEEDS TO BE MANAGED?

The basic character of reference, providing "assistance to individuals seeking information and ideas" (Bunge & Bopp, 2001, p. 6) has remained constant throughout the history of reference services. Of course the extent and nature of that assistance varies from institution to institution depending on size, mission and patrons. According to Lewis (1994), the head of public services at a major university, reference services include working with patrons at a desk, collection selection and management, liaison, bibliographic instruction and implementation of electronic services. Kibbee (1991) similarly typifies reference services as encompassing collection development, information services, user education and special collections and services. Barnello (1996) more narrowly defines the work into five categories: directions and general reference; technical assistance; information look up (ready reference); research consultation; and library instruction.

Management of the reference department includes not just the services, but also the service providers. Nofsinger and Bosch (p. 88, 1994) suggest the role of reference manager must cover three major areas: "management of reference personnel; implementation and adaptation of new technologies while maintaining traditional means of information access, and leadership and planning for anticipated changes in the future." Because more and more demands are being placed on reference staff, the job of managing them becomes more complex (Dunshire, 2001). Spalding (1990) and others state that, in addition to department level functions of coordinating activities, securing resources, serving as an advocate for the unit and otherwise providing a vital node in the communication network, reference managers must serve as a model for and mentor to individual reference staff (Nofsinger & Bosch, 1994). This includes exhibiting fair behaviors that work in support of clearly stated institutional values and job expectations, socializing to the institutional culture, providing constructive performance evaluations, and offering professional development opportunities. Because the technology integral to reference work changes at breakneck speed, the need for ongoing learning and enhancement of technical skills on the part of staff has accelerated tremendously. Professional development can be promoted internally through such actions as shared jobs, rotating job duties, project work or temporary appointments, as well as the more traditional training opportunities. Spalding (1990) also outlines the responsibilities of the individual to know her/himself and seek out those experiences that will keep her/him a valuable and engaged professional.

THE CHANGING REFERENCE LANDSCAPE

In today's often conflicting climate of simultaneous expansion and contraction, David Lewis (1994) says it is "urgent" that we change how reference services are provided even though we're not yet clear about the extent of the problems or their answers. Barnello (1996) rightly points out that many of the changes in academic libraries are responding to changes in higher education–distance education being a notable example. Others note that libraries reflect the cultural and political environment in which they exist (King et al., 1991), and certainly the proliferation of information noise in American culture is commonly acknowledged (Urgo, 2000). Almost all would agree that technological changes are having the most profound impact. Stuart and Hutto (1996) put it succinctly when they say that reference is moving from a "collection-based to a service-based orientation" (p. xiii).

In addition to all the traditional functions, successful academic reference service in the future will expand to include:

- more consultation
- more project work related to electronic services and products
- a greater emphasis on subject specialization to facilitate consultation and liaison
- a need to constantly upgrade skills, especially technical skills
- increasing demand for instruction in the use of the libraries' resources
- use of more automation and lower skilled professionals to serve patrons
- serving more remote and more diverse patrons (Lewis, 1994).

Consistent with these observations and predictions, others suggest that librarians must play a more active role in shaping the electronic interfaces between patrons and our services and products (Stuart & Hutto, 1996). Most believe that, in spite of the increasingly self-service nature of many information resources, the need for instruction and mediation services between patrons and information will be an increasing demand (Dunshire, 2001; Katz, 1997, p. xvi). One writer even suggests that, given libraries philosophical underpinnings as an educational institution dedicated to preserving an informed citizenry, "education in the use of libraries and the information resources at their disposal may be considered even more basic a service than traditional reference service . . ." (King et al., 1991, p. 38).

Not surprisingly, it is also proposed that a new mix of skills will be required in order to manage these constantly evolving services. Gordon Dunshire (2001) refers to them as "meta-skills" which will replace library-specific expertise. Papandrea (1998) comments that these changes require expanded focus on both external factors and internal factors resulting in an increasingly complex management job. Whatever the particulars, most would agree that reference services is not the place for the faint of heart or those seeking predictability (Dunshire, 2001). An added challenge comes from the increased value placed on knowledge management skills in the broader marketplace; this means that many of those who might have come to libraries fresh from their master's program are now finding it more lucrative to take jobs in the private sector. Both recruitment and retention are becoming significant concerns. Since library salaries are unlikely to increase to competitive levels in the near future, it is truer now than ever before that "management, in partnership with staff, must continually examine organizational structure and communication for their impact on professional development and satisfaction" (Spalding, 1990, p. 231).

ALTERNATIVE MODELS OF MANAGING AND ORGANIZING REFERENCE

Defined in operational terms, *management* is the act of directing and organizing to accomplish a goal. (Kibbee, 1991, p. 196)

While there is some evidence that university libraries are confined to hierarchical management structures (ARL, 1991, cited in Lewis, 1994, p. 52; Kibbee, 1991), various iterations of team and participatory management, at least in reference departments, have been tried. In general the hierarchical model, in which all authority and decisions emanate from the department head, has the advantage of efficiency. Typically less time is spent in consultation and decision-making because this model does not necessitate seeking and using input from the staff (Kibbee, 1991). A common drawback is the feeling of disenfranchisement and lowered morale among professional staff.

Both the general management and library literature promote participatory management, i.e., a greater involvement of staff in departmental or organizational decision-making. Kibbee (1991) suggests, for example, that the structure under the head of reference is comparable to a web–"a multifaceted organization, in which it is not uncommon for individual reference librarians to hold multiple responsibilities and to assume managerial roles for the administration of specific functions" (p. 193). Postulated benefits are improved morale, increased motivation and involvement, development of diverse and flexible skills, greater recognition and respect among colleagues and avoidance of burnout (Perdue & Piotrowski, 1986; Spalding, 1990). The benefits to patron/customer service are promoted as well. Potential drawbacks include the increased time required to make decisions and negative reactions when staff input is not the determining factor in major decisions.

Collective management represents the other end of the continuum; here, authority and responsibility rest with the group as a whole. Problems with accountability make this a difficult model to maintain in large departments, although it has been successfully used in at least some college settings (Comer et al., 1988, cited in Kibbee, 1991, p. 198). The advantages reported were improved morale, good staff development opportunities, greater ownership of the mission, goals and work. Drawbacks are variable levels of management skills, additional responsibility for the head of public services and a difficult decision-making process when opinions are divided.

Some specific examples of non-traditional reference management in academic libraries have been described in the literature. Gilles and Zlatos (1999) and Perdue and Piotrowski (1986), at Washington State University and West Florida, respectively, have decided to share the head of reference responsibilities by rotating tenured (or equivalently qualified) librarians through the position. In both settings, the acting reference head maintained most or all of their other librarian responsibilities. It is noteworthy that at Washington State, they do have a permanent position, Head of User Services, which would probably encompass a significant amount of the work that normally falls to a head of reference. The report does not detail the duties of the person in the 3-year rotating position so it's difficult to make direct comparisons. They go on to note that this is a facilitator position and suggest that the department operates as a team in much of the decision-making. West Florida has also been happy with their rotating reference head and notes the advantages usually cited in connection with other team-based or highly participatory models. In addition, these managerial rotations provide avenues for developing administrative skills and promoting institution-wide perspectives among staff. Potential problems noted are the lack of financial remuneration for additional responsibilities, the difficulties of balancing administrative work with other responsibilities and some individual's unsuitability for the role of management. Both articles suggest that it is essential to have a supportive group of colleagues and that the positions be voluntarily taken on. Perdue and Piotrowski (1986) also believe the size of the department might play a crucial role in the ability to use this model.

Papandrea (1998) feels the major flaw with the rotational approach is that it "does not overcome the limitations of individual weaknesses . . . or fully take advantage of individual strengths" (p. 124). She recommends instead letting people specialize in those areas in which they have the strongest interest and greatest strengths and to cross-train in other areas. This would look like a system of assistant managers, at least functionally, if not on an organizational chart. Everyone would have a slightly different job; there would be no standard or typical reference librarian.

Below the level of department head, there have also been numerous experiments with how the work in the department is organized and carried out (Bunge & Bopp, 2001; Kibbee, 1991). The Brandeis or two-tiered model is probably the most notable. Paraprofessionals offer the first point of interaction with patrons at the desk while professional librarians are available for more complex questions or lengthier consultation. Both successes and failures have been described in the literature

(Nassar, 1997). Although this model attempts to address some of the challenges to reference noted above, they don't really alter the fundamental management structure.

Other debates center around whether or not reference services should be centralized or de-centralized throughout the institution and Kibbee (1991) provides a good overview of the advantages and disadvantages of each approach.

David Lewis, Head of Public Services at the University Libraries, Indiana University-Purdue University, Indianapolis, argues compellingly for a model, which brings the programmatic and budgetary authority right down to the front line of reference in academic libraries. The current hierarchical management structures of most universities and their libraries stifle professionalism and initiative; therefore what is needed is a professional bureaucracy, more akin to the organization of a law firm. Library hierarchies should be flattened, equivalent support services must be offered at all levels, and public services planning and priority setting must be done by reference. If we are at the forefront of technological changes in information services, as we like to present ourselves, then we must adapt our organizations to support this position or risk failure. He believes that without this shift, the demands for changing the work of reference will be unrealized.

Geraldine King, who was the first chair of the Management of Reference Committee of ALA's Reference and Adult Services division, believes there is an inherent contradiction in seeking to share the workload of the reference department.

> Reference librarians are reluctant to take on managerial duties or become reference managers . . . They like being reference librarians; they like working with one client, researching a subject and hunting for information. They want someone else to solve the nitty gritty problems . . . (p. 407)

And yet, they must do so. She believes it is essential that reference managers have experience as reference professionals in order to most effectively manage the "practice of reference librarianship." Her proposed solution is for every reference librarian to take on a piece of managing the reference department, perhaps scheduling, training or a subject subdivision. One possibility is what she calls matrix management where each librarian is simultaneously being a manager in some areas and a "managee" in others. This allows the individual to still function as a reference librarian while developing other skills.

EVOLUTION OF REFERENCE ORGANIZATION
AND MANAGEMENT AT OSU

Both desire and necessity have prompted changes in the organization and management of reference services at the Oregon State University Libraries in the past 15 years. Our experiences have taught us that size matters (large groups cannot function efficiently or effectively), training in facilitation and other meeting skills does make a difference, and communication is critical. We have also confirmed that "collegiality" is a core value that overlays all of our activities and the choices we make.

Earlier models were typically hierarchical with several layers of management: office managers, assistant heads, department heads, division heads. In earlier versions we provided reference service at several different desks: sciences, social sciences and humanities, information, maps, government information, a CD center. These have been variously combined and re-aligned over the years until we reached our present configuration of a main reference/technical assistance desk and a government information, maps and microforms desk. A branch library 55 miles distant has always supported our marine sciences programs, and a new branch campus in central Oregon will share facilities and services with the local community college.

In the mid-1990s, while still retaining department heads and library-wide administrative groups, the library's public services departments formed into teams for Access, Frontline Services, Electronic Resources, and User Education. Each team was headed by a public services department head. This structure more or less overlays the traditional hierarchical structure, and the teams consisted of members from each of the public services departments. For example, the Library User Education Team included staff from Government Documents, Access, Reference, and Research Services. A Public Services Council consisting of the Associate University Librarian for Public Services, the team leaders/department heads, and a representative selected by each team coordinated the activities of the team. This initial experiment with Public Services Teams was an attempt to eliminate barriers to communication and workflow between departments, and foster staff participation in goal setting and decision-making.

Shortly after the Public Services Teams were formed, the library was integrated into Information Services (IS) along with Computing, Communication Media, and Telecommunications. A formal team structure across all units was initiated, and the library's Public Services Teams were absorbed into this larger organizational structure.

Several of the IS Teams were composed of members from what previously had been different departments throughout IS, in an effort to integrate similar functions and reduce duplication. For example, the IS Frontline Team consisted of individuals who staffed information and reception desks in all IS units. Some staff served on more than one team and all staff received extensive team training. Department heads were eliminated and replaced with team sponsors, who retained budgetary authority and responsibility for personnel assignments and evaluation. Major fiscal problems in IS eventually spelled the end of this model although former departments began re-emerging before teams officially disappeared.

Today, the Reference and Instruction (RI) Department is managed by a department head, who reports to the Associate University Librarian for Public Services and Innovative Technology, and is a member of the Library's management group. A newly designated assistant head of reference also meets with library management and leads the Reference Services Workgroup, the largest of three workgroups in the department. The department head convenes and leads the RI Council, which includes the assistant department head, the Distance Education/Outreach Services Librarian, RI's representative on the Library Web Group, liaisons from Library Technology and Collection Development, the coordinators for the Instruction and Publications/Communication Workgroups, and a member of the administrative support staff. The Council meets twice a month, alternating weeks with full RI Department meetings. The frequency of workgroup meetings varies depending on current workload; the Instruction Workgroup, for example, has been meeting three times a week throughout the summer to develop a new course-integrated instruction program for the university's freshman composition courses.

Of the three workgroups in the RI Department, the largest, Reference Services, is responsible for two service desks (Reference/Technical Assistance, and Government Information, Maps and Microforms), the print reference collections, e-mail reference, and the Information Commons. The Information Commons includes the Electronic Reference Center (32 workstations), and 64 general computing and e-mail workstations. As noted earlier, this workgroup is led by the Assistant Head of Reference, unlike the other two which have rotating coordinator positions.

The Instruction Workgroup is responsible for coordinating all aspects of the instruction program, including course-related teaching, credit courses, a web tutorial, and instructional facilities and equipment. This workgroup includes the Distance Education/Outreach Services Librarian, who provides liaison to community and school groups and the university's program for first-year students, in addition to supporting Distance and Continuing Education students. The Publications/Communication Workgroup oversees the creation and production of print and electronic publications, library information included in university publications, content of the library web's Research Gateway, and "emergency" signage. The Publications/Communications Workgroup includes RI's representative on the Library Web Group and a technical writer.

SHARED MANAGERIAL RESPONSIBILITIES: WHO DOES WHAT?

In "Roles of the Head of Reference," Nofsinger and Bosch identify three broad categories typically assigned to department heads: personnel management, implementation and adoption of new technologies, and leadership and planning for future changes (1994, p. 88). At OSU, the RI Council and workgroups either assist in, or take primary responsibility for, most of these functions.

Personnel Management

"Training and coordination" (ibid, p. 88) are shared activities. Training of new staff is coordinated by the direct supervisor, which is the department head in the case of tenure-track librarians, and other librarians or professional faculty in the case of classified and temporary staff. The actual training is developed and provided by the workgroups and individuals with specific work assignments. The department head coordinates and approves the professional development and continuing education done outside the library, usually at the request of an individual staff member or, occasionally, upon the recommendation of a workgroup. The groups represented on the Council, however, carry out the majority of in-house training and continuing education. Reference Services and Instruction Workgroups have offered sessions on such topics as case law, creating lesson plans, using the electronic classroom, and presentation skills. Additionally, the Reference Services Workgroup has developed a manual for Reference Desk procedures, trains the pool of on-call librarians who substitute at the Reference Desk, and oversees the customer service and reference-related training of the student assistants who work at the Reference Desk. Collection Development's liaison to the Council facilitates training for new electronic products, and Library

Technology's liaison has coordinated and presented workshops on web page development.

"Socialization and the corporate culture" (ibid, p. 89) is ideally a function of the department head, especially with regard to the promotion and tenure process. Other bodies in the Library support this process, including the Promotion and Tenure Committee and the Library Faculty Association's Research and Writing Group. Likewise, more senior faculty often serve as informal mentors to junior faculty. As Nofsinger and Bosch note (p. 89), the values of an organization are intangible and often an outcome of organizational history; other staff can communicate organizational history, but the department head is the person best suited to advise on how to be successful in a given environment.

A large number of tasks are included in the category, "Supervision and daily operations" (ibid, p. 89). Groups represented on the Council do some of these, and some remain the purview of the department head. For example, scheduling of the service desks, implementing new services, collecting data for evaluation, reporting on progress for projects, and development of procedure manuals are all carried out by the workgroups. Monitoring the budget, making final determinations of staff workload, monitoring personnel behaviors and attitudes, and some reporting out of departmental work remain primarily with the department head and assistant department head.

"Communication" (ibid, p. 89) is also a shared function. Workgroup coordinators are expected to move information back and forth between their members and the Council, which of course includes the department head. Council meetings serve to facilitate coordination between the workgroups, committees and departments interfacing with reference. Primary responsibility for communicating between reference and other areas of the library, including administration, is the duty of the department head.

"Performance evaluation," which Nofsinger and Bosch call "the most sensitive area of communication," (1994, p. 90) is also shared, to an extent, in that all members of the department provide feedback regarding their co-workers, on the basis of their work at the reference desks, in workgroups, and, via a peer observation process, in instruction. Ultimately, the head of reference integrates this information into both a written and oral presentation for the individual and ties it to an annual review and work plan.

Nofsinger and Bosch also speak to managing "conflict and stress" (ibid, p. 90) as a primary role for the department head. Certainly, the department head is responsible for the emotional health of the department and, as noted above, monitors personnel behaviors and attitudes. Council and the workgroups address these areas by coordinating and assigning pieces of work to assure equitable workloads. The workgroups provide small-group forums for problem solving and decision-making, addressing a frequent contributor to stress: perceived lack of control. As an example, in 2000 those working on the reference desks advocated for, and were given, approval to hire a pool of substitute reference librarians, thus relieving librarians of the need to continually add to already heavy work assignments when colleagues were absent. Members of several workgroups were involved in the recruitment, interviewing and training of our substitutes. As mentioned earlier, we rely on a strong departmental sense of collegiality and mutual commitment to service quality.

Technology Facilitator

Although the head of reference is nominally responsible for the Information Commons, the area in which many of the new technologies are made available and utilized, a number of other groups share the workload.

"Utilization of technologies" (ibid, p. 92) related to user access to information resources is supported by the Library Technology Department, which installs and maintains CD resources, production software, and computers in the Information Commons and classrooms which provide access to resources. The Electronic Resources Librarian and subject librarians, through Collection Development, decide on which resources to prioritize for purchase.

"Development of staff expertise" (ibid, p. 93) is shared by all RI workgroups and library departments. For example, the Reference Services Workgroup sponsored training in legal reference, Library Technology conducted HTML and web editor training, and the Instruction Workgroup offered workshops on lesson design. All play a part in facilitating professional development and in helping to keep staff current in new technologies, products and services.

Various workgroups share in the "assessment of user needs" (ibid, p. 94) by collecting statistics, evaluating classes, and tracking use of electronic resources. Via the Council, the constantly shifting demands for services can be coordinated and prioritized and recommendations made to the department head for new equipment, service hours, level of staffing, and so forth. The department head is responsible for coordinating such equipment and service requests vis à vis the current budget.

Leading for Future Change

Ideally, the head of reference will lead as well as manage, providing strategic direction for the department and the library. The input of Council, both during meetings and from documentation created in the workgroups, helps frame these strategic decisions. Recently the Instruction Workgroup created a mission and goals statement that served as a model in a department-wide retreat. Reference Services is currently refining a similar document. The assistant head of reference chairs an Information Commons Visioning Group that is developing a mission statement to help guide future priorities and services. The department as a whole will determine our priorities based on these documents and general discussions in meetings and retreats. In the other direction, the department head works with the Council to determine how to implement strategic decisions made at the administrative and institutional levels.

THE ADVANTAGES OF ORGANIZING AND MANAGING THIS WAY

Clearly, our model is a version of participatory management and, as Papandrea has advocated, "shares the burden, shares the power and shares the fun" (1998, p. 124). It caters to people's strengths and interests. It provides opportunities for people to more fully develop management and leadership skills. A larger number of people are more familiar with the priorities and processes involved in coordinating the functioning of a large department than had been the case in previous models. Council members who were interviewed attest to the broadened perspective provided by that role. Those who write about professional development for reference librarians are virtually unanimous in promoting participatory management as an effective mechanism for this (Fulton, 1990; Spalding, 1990). King (1987) and Katz (1986) also believe that having staff manage portions of the work brings the essential front line perspective of reference librarians to the management of those services. Another advantage is that the department head has multiple perspectives from which to draw. Ridgeway (1986) notes that the typical conditions of managing reference are antithetical to creativity; however, one creativity technique is brainstorming and the Council provides a forum for this.

Several authors have spoken of the necessity for sharing and shifting work to avoid burnout (Bunge & Bopp, 2001; Jones & Reichel, 1986). It is important that individuals have the opportunity to move in and out of levels of responsibility for a time, depending on other career demands; an example in our situation is allowing people to step out of Council positions to meet obligations related to getting tenure. When interviewed, staff are unequivocal in their support of the workgroup structure as the most effective way to get things done. People can be involved in areas that interest them and the groups are small enough to be focused and productive. Most believe there is simply too much work for a single person to be responsible for.

Flexibility is an advantage from the perspective of organizational responsiveness as well. Our model allows us to add or subtract members from Council as needed, to address both departmental and service needs. For example, as we plan for library services at a new branch campus, the reference librarian on the library-wide planning group meets with the Council.

Dixie Jones (1997) tells us that to have excellent reference service, we must have a collegial and well-functioning team. Our model fosters several of the factors she identifies as contributing to creating an effective team: communication, feeling included, and having strengths and contributions recognized. Finally, opportunities to participate meaningfully in departmental decision-making could potentially serve as a powerful recruitment and retention tool in an era of increasing competition for qualified staff.

CAUTIONARY NOTES

There are always potential downsides to any organizational model. Concerns expressed in interviews with staff and faculty include a continuing perception of communication problems. Comments suggest that information is perceived as getting stuck in Council and not always passed on to the department in general. As one staff member said, the existence of the Council "can make it feel like communication has taken place when it really hasn't." Others would like to see mechanisms for more regular communication from the rest of the department to the Council. To facilitate communication, workgroups have begun posting minutes of their meetings on the library's intranet. Our acting head of reference also implemented a brief but popular "This Week in Reference and Instruction" newsletter sent to the entire library staff. In a related concern, the department head was, until recently, solely responsible for channeling communication to and from the library administration and other managers. Now, the assistant head also meets with administrators and managers, relieving the department head of some of the burden while still not overwhelming administration.

If some people are more included by being on the Council, others may feel more excluded. One of the ways we have addressed this is by allowing flexibility in the membership of the various workgroups, which in turn can result in changes in coordinators who participate in the Council meetings. Another strategy instituted in the last year has been to have half- or full-day departmental retreats where we discuss common goals, identify departmental priorities and plan future services.

During one of our earlier organizational iterations, the Office Manager position was eliminated. Many felt this was a major error in terms of staff productivity. Even with our current model, there remained a pressing need for this level of administrative support, so we lobbied for and achieved reinstatement of a full-time position.

As noted by Perdue and Piotrowski (1986), there is the risk that people will not want to take on the extra responsibilities and/or time commitments when there is no financial incentive to do so. To date we have not found that to be a problem. We agree that it is important to make positions on Council voluntary as much as possible. However, certain essential functions need to be represented in the communication and decision-making process; therefore, some positions cannot be voluntary because there is only one person who can serve.

There is always the concern that people who are not particularly skilled in communicating, coordinating or leading will be put in positions that require these skills. Fortunately, nearly all staff have participated in extensive team training, resulting in a high percentage of people with leadership and facilitation skills. We have also found that strong workgroup members and a strong department head can mentor those who feel they are not ready to take on these roles. The fact that most of these positions are not permanent and that many of them are rotated mitigates these risks. Council exposes members to several models of leading, coordinating, and facilitating. Although there are never guarantees that you can develop someone into an effective manager, at least the opportunities are offered.

A major concern is that workgroup coordinators and other members of Council are often given responsibility without accompanying authority, which can slow down project implementation, especially when other library departments are involved. We will be hiring a new head of Reference soon, having been without a regular full-time person for over a year, and the hope is that s/he will be in a better position to advocate on behalf of Council-identified projects and issues.

CONCLUSION

As with other organizations confronted by changing external demands, libraries must find more flexible and responsive organizational structures than the traditional hierarchies (Papandrea, 1998). Through trial and error we have arrived at a working model for managing reference services that provides this flexibility. Our Council and workgroup arrangement truly provides the opportunity for the entire Reference and Instruction "village" to be involved and share in the increasingly complex job of managing an ever-expanding array of services. It provides professional development opportunities for staff and brings the frontline perspective to decisions affecting our work. Our model may be more difficult to implement in a setting that does not have such a strong history of teamwork and collegial staff relations; certainly this model will not work for everyone. We acknowledge that there are potential pitfalls, but have found that these can be mitigated if attention is paid. For us, this model incorporates many of the advantages of participatory management while avoiding many of its problems.

REFERENCES

Barnello, Inga H. (1996), "The Changing Face of Reference: A History of the Future," in *The Changing Face of Reference*, edited by Lynne M. Stuart and Dena Holiman Hutto. Greenwich, CT: JAI Press, Inc., 3-17.

Bunge, Charles A. and Richard E. Bopp. (2001), "History and Varieties of Reference Services," in *Reference and Information Services: An Introduction, 3rd Ed.*, edited by Richard E. Bopp and Linda C. Smith. Englewood, CO: Libraries Unlimited, Inc., 3-27.

Fulton, Tara Lynn (1990), "Mentor Meets Telemachus: The Role of the Department Head in Orienting and Inducting the Beginning Reference Librarian," *The Reference Librarian* 30, 257-273.

Jones, Carl and Mary Reichel (1986), "Burnout and the Reference Manager," in *Improving Reference Management*, edited by Trish Ridgeway, Peggy Cover and Carl Stone. Chicago: American Library Association, 35-43.

Jones, Dixie (1997), "Plays Well with Others, or the Importance of Collegiality Within a Reference Unit," *The Reference Librarian* 59, 163-175.

Katz, Ruth (1986), "Introduction to the Workshop," in *Improving Reference Management*, edited by Trish Ridgeway, Peggy Cover and Carl Stone. Chicago: American Library Association, 1-5.

King, Geraldine (1987), "The Management of Reference Services," *RQ* 26 (Spring), 407-409.

Lewis, David W. (1994), "Making Academic Reference Services Work," *College & Research Libraries* 55, n.5, 445-456.

Nofsinger, Mary M., and Bosch, Allan W. (1994), "Roles of the Head of Reference: From the 1990s to the 21st Century," *The Reference Librarian* 43, 87-99.

Papandrea, Virginia A. (1998), "Managing Reference Services in the Electronic Age: A Competing Values Approach to Effectiveness," *The Reference Librarian* 60, 111-126.

Perdue, Bob and Piotrowski, Chris (1986), "Supervisory Rotation: Impact on an Academic Library Reference Staff," *RQ* 25 (Spring), 361-365.

Ridgeway, Trish (1986), "Creativity and Innovation in Reference Management," in *Improving Reference Management*, edited by Trish Ridgeway, Peggy Cover and Carl Stone. Chicago: American Library Association, 55-70.

Spalding, Helen H. (1990), "The Developing Reference Librarian: An Administrative Perspective," *The Reference Librarian* 30, 225-236.

The 21st Century Reference Department: Working to Provide Quality Service to Users

Patience L. Simmonds

SUMMARY. Reference service in academic libraries has evolved over the years from what was the "reference interview" to the kind of service transaction which takes many forms and involves numerous information resources and the highest librarian expertise in some situations. Reference is more versatile now than ever, and this may be attributed to the abundance of resources and the multitude of ways librarians can acquire access to needed information. Coordination of efforts, expertise, and resources can make a great reference department function efficiently and effectively. College and university libraries with huge reference departments may need reference managers or heads of reference to manage them, but there are smaller libraries with small reference departments which employ less than five reference librarians. Managing these small libraries with an even smaller pool of reference librarians may not seem as complicated as managing large ones.

The head of reference position is an important one in the library, both for the staff and for the users served. This article will try to present views on the qualities, qualifications, and requirements which the head of reference should possess in the 21st century. *[Article copies available for a fee from The Haworth Document Delivery Service: 1-800-HAWORTH. E-mail address: <docdelivery@haworthpress.com> Website: <http://www.Haworth Press.com> © 2003 by The Haworth Press, Inc. All rights reserved.]*

Patience L. Simmonds is Assistant Librarian, Penn State Erie, The Behrend College, The John M. Lilley Library, 5091 Station Road, Erie, PA 16563 (E-mail: pls7@psu.edu).

[Haworth co-indexing entry note]: "The 21st Century Reference Department: Working to Provide Quality Service to Users." Simmonds, Patience L. Co-published simultaneously in *The Reference Librarian* (The Haworth Information Press, an imprint of The Haworth Press, Inc.) No. 81, 2003, pp. 89-103; and: *Managing the Twenty-First Century Reference Department: Challenges and Prospects* (ed: Kwasi Sarkodie-Mensah) The Haworth Information Press, an imprint of The Haworth Press, Inc., 2003, pp. 89-103. Single or multiple copies of this article are available for a fee from The Haworth Document Delivery Service [1-800-HAWORTH, 9:00 a.m. - 5:00 p.m. (EST). E-mail address: docdelivery@haworthpress.com].

http://www.haworthpress.com/store/product.asp?sku=J120
© 2003 by The Haworth Press, Inc. All rights reserved.
10.1300/J120v39n81_08

KEYWORDS. Academic libraries, 21st century reference departments, reference service, instruction, reference librarians, paraprofessionals in reference, head of reference, library use

REFERENCE SERVICE AND THE STATE OF LIBRARIES

"Libraries are changing." This is a statement that resounds in much of the library literature, and it is supposed to alert libraries and librarians to the developments that are taking place in the 21st century and prepare them to be ready to tackle users' needs and expectations. Denise Troll states that libraries are changing in response to changes in the learning and research environment and changes in the behavior of users (Troll, 2002).[1] If libraries are indeed changing, then librarians and the departments they work in must also change to meet users' needs. Goble states that "change is not new to librarians. What is different is that change is no longer intermittent. It is constant and its pace is fast accelerating" (Goble, 1997).[2] As libraries continue to change, many people including librarians wonder what is in store for libraries venturing into the 21st century. Academic libraries cannot prepare effectively for the future or position themselves on campus until they understand their changing roles in the current learning and research environment, which is radically different from the environment a decade ago (Troll, 2002).[3] The provision of good reference service in any library is central to the effectiveness of that particular library. Reference service has evolved over the decades, and the importance of reference service has dramatically shifted from just the centrality of emphasis of the "reference interview," to a more complex nature of the kind of transaction, which takes many forms and involves numerous information resources and the highest librarian expertise in some situations. Smith suggests that librarians need to recognize that this new environment has created a plethora of choices for end-users, and that if academic librarians hope to compete successfully in the information marketplace, they will have to restructure reference service (Smith, 122).[4]

Knowledge and expertise of the reference staff, a great reference collection, different formats of information access, effective communication, and easy availability of reference assistance when needed are among some of the ingredients in the makeup of a great reference department. The change in the organization and delivery of reference service could probably be attributed to the abundance of resources and the multitude of ways librarians can acquire access to needed information.

Reference service in academia is also more versatile now than ever, and no single reference librarian can claim absolute expertise in how it should be organized or be conducted. Teaching faculty, students and staff as well as the public expect quality reference service. These patrons expect this quality to come not only from the reference collection and the other resources acquired by the library, but also from the people who provide instruction and reference service to them. Patrons demand reference service from both traditional and non-traditional sources. Reference departments are now providing traditional reference service, plus a definite increase in electronic and digital reference service. Most libraries also provide virtual, electronic and digital reference service, including telephone and e-mail service to their users. Another reason for the increase in the use of electronic and digital reference services by the library users could also be because of the constitution of our users. The users are familiar with the multitude of resources available on the Web, and they are used to demanding and receiving instant gratification while sitting in the comfort of their homes and dormitory rooms. There are those users who are completely remote and we will never be able to identify them with any of our traditional user characteristics, other than the fact that they need information and they need it fast. Many college and university libraries are required to provide service to distance education users. With many colleges and universities having distance education programs, the services of libraries are stretched to accommodate the needs of as many users as possible.

REFERENCE PERSONNEL

The people who work in reference departments play an important role in providing quality service to the library's clientele. Ruth Katz describes reference work as a team sport where team reference needs managers who have been players (Katz, 1986).[5] The person who manages the whole department can contribute immensely to the overall effectiveness of the reference department. In the same vein, that particular person in many ways can undermine the effectiveness of that department in particular, and the library in general, by initiating or instituting policies and characteristics which will be counterproductive.

Who is the best person to head or manage a reference department? In some libraries, the head of reference positions are staffed by people with no library or reference experience. Library administrators in their requirements for that kind of position, focus more on other qualifications such as effective communication, interpersonal skills, supervisory and management skills or experience, and the ability to work well with other people and empower them to be productive. Some do not require an MLS degree, or a graduate degree in a second subject area. Most reference librarians who provide reference service in academic libraries also teach library instruction to the students. They get the chance to come into contact with the users both during instruction classes and at the reference desk. In some libraries, both librarians and paraprofessionals also provide reference.

OVERVIEW OF THE REFERENCE DEPARTMENT

Most reference departments in academic libraries are often centrally located. They are the first places users normally approach for assistance when they enter the library. There are different types of reference departments. Some libraries have well-organized reference departments, which are also responsible for library instruction. Other small or medium-sized libraries provide good reference service, but do not have a formal reference department. In such libraries, reference librarians are responsible for coordinating reference service and may be supervised by the overall head of the library. The jobs of reference and instruction coordination are subsequently divided among the reference librarians in those institutions.

An example of a medium-sized library where there is no formal or designated reference department is The John M. Lilley Library at Penn State Erie, which provides service to a student population of approximately 3,700 plus students, 218 full-time, and 82 part-time faculty in four schools: business, engineering and engineering technology, humanities and social sciences, and science. The Lilley Library has a book collection of about 102,000 volumes. The library is part of the Penn State University Libraries and has a total number of three reference librarians and the director of the library. The library does not have a reference department or head of reference. The director makes decisions about issues relating to reference service provision. Reference desk schedules are also developed and coordinated by the director of the library with input from the reference librarians and the paraprofessionals who work at the reference desk. Reference librarians and the director select the reference materials for all subject areas, and a reference librarian selected by the director coordinates the reference selection and tabulation of all reference acquisitions for collection building. The same reference librarians provide instruction classes to the student users. Like the procedure in the provision of reference service, a librarian is selected to coordinate instruction requests from faculty and distribute the classes among the three librarians.

Other libraries have large reference departments with many librarians responsible for different subjects areas–some of these even have other subject librarians reporting directly to them.

Various names are used in the literature and in libraries, especially in academic libraries to describe position titles in reference. Among these are:

- Head of Reference and Instruction Services
- Head of Central Reference
- Reference Manager
- Head/Coordinator of Reference/Reference Services
- Head of Reference/Public Services
- Head of Information Services.

There are college and university libraries with huge reference departments and these often need reference managers or heads of reference to manage them. There are also smaller libraries with small reference departments, which employ less than five reference librarians. Managing these small libraries with an even smaller pool of reference librarians may not seem as complicated as managing large ones. Coordination of efforts, experience, expertise, and resources can make a great reference department function efficiently and effectively. Every reference department deserves a great head of reference to manage it and work with the reference staff to provide the best service to its users. The user does not see what goes on beyond the reference desk and the collection, and may not be aware of all the duties performed by the librarians and the other paraprofessionals. What he or she is aware of are the resources and services available to him or her. A well-organized reference department is important for the proper functioning of the library and the provision of quality reference service to the library's users. More demands are being made on library personnel in all departments, and reference is no exception. Many reference departments have reorganized their departments to accommodate new modes of information delivery and accessibility.

The head of reference should be responsible for spearheading the organization of the department and setting in place proper channels of authority and responsibility in the department. There should be a clear delineation of who is responsible for what jobs in the department. Nothing gets accomplished if the head of reference does not identify specific people for specific jobs and hold them responsible for completing these jobs.

REFERENCE MANAGERS /HEAD OF REFERENCE

This author believes that a person hired as a head of reference needs to have reference qualifications that should include a strong background and experience in reference and instruction, and a basic knowledge about librarianship. A head of reference with no grounding in reference and instruction will not do well in the long run in that particular position. A reference librarian can be an effective head of reference. He or she is capable of learning supervisory and managerial skills in order to function in this position. A review of some recent head of reference position announcements found that a head of reference should have the following requirements: an MLS degree, a second master's degree, an advanced degree, professional and/or on-the-job training and experience, excellent communication skills and effective interpersonal skills, among other qualifications. The head of reference in the 21st century will have to be capable of handling some of the new skills which the computer age has forced librarians and paraprofessionals to quickly acquire. She has to be familiar with new technologies that are required to provide access to information for the library user.

Typical advertisements for reference managers and head of reference positions normally state the following:

- required qualifications
- desired qualifications
- job responsibilities
- salary
- tenure/rank/ faculty status
- reporting lines
- desired skills or experiences
- desired educational experiences.

What role does the reference department play in the library? In academia, students and faculty saw the reference desk and the department which controls the desk as the focal point for providing answers to their research questions. Some users expect to see reference librarians seated at the desk waiting for their inquiries. Even though the Web has opened many other avenues for providing information to users, the reference desk is still the place where users first stop to ask for information. When they require information online, many users still expect remote service from the reference librarians.

A lot more goes on beyond the reference desk. Reference librarians, heads of reference, and other people who work in the reference department are supposed to work together to make the department and the desk very functional for the students and faculty. Susan DiMattis recommends that a head of a department should develop a mission statement and a list of goals for the department, and that she and her staff should work as a team with the same purpose, and focus time and energy on those things that are most important (DiMattis,1996).[6] Cooperation and collaboration among the people who work in reference can help facilitate the transition of the reference department into the 21st century not only for themselves, but also for their primary clientele. How would they learn to adjust to the changing technology? How would they learn new technologies and use of new electronic and digital resources so they can effectively transfer that knowledge to their users?

LITERATURE REVIEW

In trying to write this article, this author reviewed library literature in order to find out what the people in the field are saying about the role that reference managers or heads of reference play in libraries in the 21st century. There was available evidence in the literature, which showed that there is a need for a change in reference service provision during the 21st century. The library literature reflects this and emphasizes the role of the head of reference as the person who will plan and direct reference library policy, programs and procedures. Gary White's article examines head of reference positions from 1990-1999, and analyzes job qualifications, desired educational qualifications and desired skills or experience. He states that the most frequently cited requirements for heads of reference positions were communication or interpersonal skills and the MLS degree. He also states that the most frequently cited desired educational qualification was a second master's degree (White, 2000).[7] In commenting on reference services for the 21st century, Jo Bell Whitlatch states that in using Web information sources for reference services, librarians face two important challenges: (1) locating and utilizing high quality information sources when answering user queries; and (2) educating users concerning the need to critically evaluate information sources obtained from the Web (Whitlatch, Spring 1999).[8] The vast amount of information accessible to users confound many people who try to weave through all that information.

HEAD OF REFERENCE RESPONSIBILITIES

Regular responsibilities of a head of reference would include, among other things, administrative and supervisory duties. She is responsible for distributing reference duties in the department, ensuring that everything which the reference personnel do contributes to the department and the library's effectiveness. She coordinates the reference department's mission with that of the library's overall mission to meet the needs of the users. The administrative and supervisory duties, which the head of reference performs, are essential to the existence of the reference department. The very effectiveness of what the students and faculty depend on to utilize the resources of a good reference department depends on the expertise, knowledge and communication skills of the people who provide the day-to-day reference service.

The head of reference also evaluates the performance of the librarians in the department. In some academic libraries, the head of reference is also the person responsible for the library's instruction program and has both the reference and instruction librarians reporting to her. The way the head of reference organizes her department, executes her duties, communicates her mission and vision for the department to the people she works with, can help make or break a reference department. The users do not see the background work, which the person in charge performs. All they see is the service that is provided to them and the reference resources available to them. The administrative or supervisory experience of the person in charge of the department is more important to the reference and instruction librarians and paraprofessionals who work in the reference department. The head of reference depends on the work performed by the reference personnel to make the work she performs useful for the users.

What do the reference departments/reference librarians need from the head of reference? What does the head of Reference need to do to be ready to provide reference service in the 21st century? What skills would be needed to manage the reference department and work with the other personnel in the department to provide the service needed?

The head of reference should do the following things:

- Provide a well-documented mission and vision statement for the department
- Acquire a great selection of qualified reference librarians
- Include librarians in the decision-making process involving the reference department
- Put in place a policy for selecting and providing adequate and continuous training for paraprofessionals doing reference work
- Formulate uniform procedures for performing duties in the department
- Emphasize the importance of effective communication to all personnel in the department
- Provide well-defined written policies pertaining to reference and instruction (if instruction is part of the reference department)
- Be flexible but firm about issues relating to the department
- Be knowledgeable about the day-to-day work the reference librarians perform
- Be conversant with the overall work of the librarians you are evaluating
- Know the needs of the librarians
- Foster interpersonal relations among reference librarians and other staff in the reference department
- Know what the needs and expectations of the users are
- Emphasize issues important to reference librarians and users
- Perform evaluations that can help the reference personnel learn from their experiences
- Schedule regular meetings to discuss issues related to reference service.

The head of reference should refrain from doing the following things:

- Making unilateral decisions about the reference department
- Making ad hoc changes within the reference department and not explaining decisions
- Intimidating the reference staff by using "the boss card"
- Using e-mail as the primary mode of communication, thereby eroding the already limited interaction among the people in the department and library as a whole
- Assigning staff to the Reference Desk without training

- Creating busywork for librarians by asking for unnecessary assignments that are not relevant to the provision of service to the user
- "Managing" the reference personnel.

WORK CLIMATE IN THE REFERENCE DEPARTMENT

The designated coordinator or head of the reference department has the responsibility to ensure that the climate in the department is conducive to providing the best service to the users. This climate should also enable those who work in the department to be able to feel comfortable with the environment in which they work and the people with whom they work. The head of reference can take some responsibility if the climate in the department prevents the staff from doing their job. A good, firm, yet flexible head with the ability to garner the trust, confidence, and abilities of the staff can produce an environment where people will be happy to perform their best. She can envision for the staff, what and how the workplace environment should function, and then allow them to show creativity as to how that vision can be individualized in the department. The reference staff should be aware of the policies and expectations required from all the people who work there. There should be no exceptions to department policies.

Reference service is a learning process for both the person who provides the service and the beneficiary of that service. In order to be prepared for changes in the way that reference service is provided in the academic library, the reference librarians must work closely with the staff that provides the service when the reference librarian is not available. It is not a matter of competition or an ego trip. The users expect great service and that is what the reference personnel should provide. In some academic libraries, the reference librarians work very closely with the teaching faculty to ascertain the present and future needs of the students. They consult copies of faculty syllabi available either online or at the circulation desk. Most reference librarians who provide reference service also teach library instruction classes. Consulting the course syllabi helps them both in providing great instruction and reference service. They know what the students are studying in their classrooms. Once they are equipped with this kind of information, they can help the staff that also provides reference service become better prepared. In some libraries, the reference personnel provide information on topics students are currently researching, with sources for other reference personnel to consult. This is an instance where enhancing instruction can help the reference staff provide great reference through knowledge sharing and expertise. Effective communication among the people who provide reference is also very desirable.

REFERENCE LIBRARIANS AND HEAD OF REFERENCE WORKING RELATIONSHIP

Dawson and McCook assert that reference librarians in public service will continue their roles but with new demands to be proactive and technologically astute (Dawson and McCook, 1996).[9] It can be extremely overwhelming for the reference librarian to keep on top of all the new technologies and the resources that are currently available for consultation in order to satisfy the demands of the user. The head of reference that has reference experience will have to remember the stress a reference librarian can be under when requests are coming from everywhere. The head of reference basically supervises the reference librarians, and they would definitely regard in an unfavorable light the head of reference who does not know how to perform the duties they as reference librarians are required to perform. Another problem that can rear its head is the fact that an ineffective head of reference is the person who performs the evaluation for the reference librarians in the department. This can turn into a fairness and respect issue.

The academic reference librarian deals not only with her recognized primary clientele (faculty and students in the academic community), but everybody else who has access to a computer, and who can e-mail or call a reference librarian because they can get the name and the address from a library's Web site. The reference librarian needs time and appropriate resources and the ability to continue to stretch in order to satisfy the users.

REFERENCE LIBRARIANS' AND PARAPROFESSIONALS' WORKING RELATIONSHIP AT THE DESK

In libraries where paraprofessionals are required to staff the reference desk, the reference librarians should provide the paraprofessionals with continuous education and training so that they can, in turn, provide the best reference service they are capable of delivering. They should lobby to open for the paraprofessionals some of the same training opportunities available to librarians to continue to keep up with innovations in technology. There should be a show of genuine respect and appreciation for the work of all reference personnel.

Respect, empowerment, knowledge sharing, preparation, continuous training and effective communication are among some of the desirable qualities which can help prepare reference personnel for dealing with reference provision in the 21st century. Even reference librarians who think that they have the qualifications and training to perform their reference duties are now realizing that they have to be always on top of the immense and ever-changing resources. There is always a new resource that the reference personnel have to learn so they can in turn teach the users.

Some paraprofessionals possess excellent technological skills, and these can come in handy when they are combined with the research knowledge which the librarians possess. With training in reference work and sharing of knowledge among librarians and paraprofessionals, all who work in the reference department can collaborate to provide the kind of service which is demanded by our users for the 21st century.

USERS, REFERENCE LIBRARIANS AND THE HEAD OF REFERENCE

Dawson and McCook assert that "on the frontlines reference librarians are called upon to accommodate users with different levels of demands. More than ever before reference staff need to know what is 'out there' and work to provide access that fits each user's needs. The reference librarian of today must understand what is possible, work to recognize the diversity of user needs and activate technologies for users" (Dawson and McCook, 1996).[10]

Users, reference department staff and the head of reference can all collaborate to ensure that the reference department and the provision of quality reference service is the hallmark of service in any library. Changes initiated in the 21st century reference department will have to be focused more on the needs of the user. Wilson asserts that "librarians in the future will need to be flexible, adaptable, and conversant with how the new individualistic and egalitarian user seeks and uses information" (Wilson, 2000).[11] The library will have to identify the users and then assess their needs so the best service can be provided for them. The relationship among the reference personnel and the users will have to be reestablished to place the user and her expectations and needs back in the center of the library's mission and vision.

The reference personnel will also have to be more approachable and proactive towards the user.

Many users are afraid to approach librarians, and there is nothing wrong with following up on a user and asking her if she found the information she was looking for. This makes for good user service. This may sometimes seem difficult since it is harder to gauge the needs of the remote users of our reference services. Reference librarians in academia can study the needs of their students and faculty through surveys and other methods of user assessment. They can also use the faculty to reach the students. In some libraries, the reference and instruction librarians target their instruction sessions not only at the students, but also at the teaching faculty. Workshops and seminars are specifically organized for the teaching faculty to orient them to the multitude of library resources constantly being introduced into libraries. Once the faculty members are made aware of what is available, they are more likely to develop assignments for which the students can utilize the library's resources. The head of reference, and the reference and instruction librarians can work together with the faculty to learn what the future needs of the students would be when they approach the reference desk both physically or remotely.

CONCLUSION AND RECOMMENDATIONS

The 21st century is here, and reference service has already changed. No library can continue to provide reference the way it was provided even five years ago. Library resources are being improved all of the time. The changes continue to pleasantly surprise and overwhelm reference librarians as they continue to strive to make reference service available to their users. The head of reference can empower and encourage the creative skills of all of the people who work for her. She can make available the funds needed for people to get training to keep up with technological innovations in librarianship.

Reference librarians can improve reference service by providing better and more effective instruction to the students. Tenopir and Ennis, in their survey of reference librarians in 1997, reported that almost all of their respondents "admitted the need for more instruction, and more intense instruction" (Tenopir and Ennis, Nov./Dec. 1998).[12] Many students in academia are already Web savvy. They know how to navigate the Web using various search engines. What they lack is the ability to do library research, find appropriate resources and evaluate these resources. Easy access to Web technology and the fact that many students in academic institutions are given some form of library instruction may account for the decline in reference statistics which many libraries report. It is safe to assume that in some libraries, great instruction may account for fewer users approaching the reference desk for service.

Within the John M. Lilley Library at Penn State Erie, professors who bring their students in for instruction are encouraged to schedule a follow-up instruction class for the students. This enables both the teaching faculty and the librarian to help the students with their hands-on sessions when they are working on their assignments. Helping students individually with their assignments in a controlled environment equips them with the skills they need to use the library's resources in the future. Before a scheduled instruction class, the librarian can meet with the faculty member and discuss all aspects of the students' assignment and other related issues. The librarian can consult the class syllabus to see what other topics the students are studying. In some academic libraries, all of the syllabi are placed together in a folder at the circulation desk, or they can be consulted on the Web site of the various schools or departments. Instruction can be improved by working with the teaching faculty to anticipate what the students will need later on in the semester.

Reference service in the 21st century may be changing, but reference librarians, heads of reference, users, and all personnel who work in the reference department in particular, and the library in general to help to provide reference and instruction, can work together to meet the new challenges.

REFERENCES

1. Troll, Dennis, "How and Why Libraries Are Changing" Portal: *Libraries and the Academy,* Vol. 2 No. 1 (2002), pp. 99-123.

2. Goble, Davis S. "Managing in a Change Environment: From Coping to Comfort" *Library Administration & Management* Vol. 11 No. 3 Summer, 1997, pp. 151-156.

3. Troll, Dennis, "How and Why Libraries Are Changing" Portal: *Libraries and the Academy,* Vol. 2 No. 1 (2002), pp. 99-123.

4. Smith, Rebecca, "Product Management: A New Skill for Reference Librarians" *Reference & User Services Quarterly* Vol. 39 No. 3 Winter 1999, pp. 121-127.

5. Katz, Ruth M., "Improving Reference Management: Introduction to the Workshop" Ridgeway, Trish, Peggy Cover, and Carl Stone, eds., (1986) *Improving Reference Management* Reference and Adult Services Division ALA, 1986, pp. 3.

6. DiMattis, Susan, "I Am in Heaven Now, or Six Months in Hell: How to Thrive as a New Department Head" *UNABASHED Librarian* Nov. 10, 1996, pp. 27-28.

7. White, Gary, "Head of Reference Positions in Academic Libraries: A Survey of Job Announcements from 1990 through 1999," *Reference and User Services Quarterly* Vol. 39 No. 3 (Spring 2000), pp. 265-272.

8. Whitlatch, Jo Bell, "Enhancing The Quality of Reference Services for the 21st Century: Part 3" *Reference & User Services* Vol. 38 No. 3 (Spring 1999), pp. 233-234.

9. Dawson, Alma & Kathleen de la Pena McCook "Trends Affecting Roles of Reference Librarians" In *The Roles of Reference Librarians: Today and Tomorrow*, edited by Kathleen Low, The Haworth Press, Inc., 1996, pp. 53-74.

10. Ibid., pp. 53-74.

11. Wilson, Myoung C. "Evolution or Entropy? The Changing Reference Culture and The Future of Reference Librarians" In *Digital Reference in the New Millennium: Planning, Management, and Evaluation*, edited by R. David Lankes, John W. Collins, and Abby S. Kasowitz, pp. 47-57.

12. Tenopir, Carol & Lisa Ennis, "The Impact of Digital Reference on Librarians and Library Users" *Online* 22 (Nov/Dec 1998): 84-88.

Leadership or Management: Expectations for Head of Reference Services in Academic Libraries

Felix E. Unaeze

SUMMARY. This paper considers leadership and management issues affecting libraries in general. Specific attention is devoted to academic libraries and their reference departments. It focuses on the dynamics of leadership and management of academic library reference services and what is expected of the reference department head of the 21st century. It explores the changing roles of reference librarians and those of their leaders or department heads. It examines the leadership skills, traits, and competencies and attributes expected of the department head of reference in the new millennium. The paper also examines the paradox of leadership and management and draws distinction between the two terms. It finally looks into whether it is appropriate to have a manager from outside the library profession to be the head of an academic library reference department. *[Article copies available for a fee from The Haworth Document Delivery Service: 1-800-HAWORTH. E-mail address: <docdelivery@ haworthpress.com> Website: <http://www.HaworthPress.com> © 2003 by The Haworth Press, Inc. All rights reserved.]*

KEYWORDS. Leadership, management, reference department head, reference services, new millennium, 21st century, organization, organizational effectiveness, effective leader, leadership skills, leadership traits

Felix E. Unaeze is Director of Public Services, Douglas Library, Chicago State University, 9501 South King Drive, Chicago, IL 60628 (E-mail: funaeze@csu.edu). He also serves as Library Liaison to the College of Business at the same university.

[Haworth co-indexing entry note]: "Leadership or Management: Expectations for Head of Reference Services in Academic Libraries." Unaeze, Felix E. Co-published simultaneously in *The Reference Librarian* (The Haworth Information Press, an imprint of The Haworth Press, Inc.) No. 81, 2003, pp. 105-117; and: *Managing the Twenty-First Century Reference Department: Challenges and Prospects* (ed: Kwasi Sarkodie-Mensah) The Haworth Information Press, an imprint of The Haworth Press, Inc., 2003, pp. 105-117. Single or multiple copies of this article are available for a fee from The Haworth Document Delivery Service [1-800-HAWORTH, 9:00 a.m. - 5:00 p.m. (EST). E-mail address: docdelivery@haworthpress.com].

INTRODUCTION

Leadership and management have always been used repeatedly in the human resource industry and often discussed when selecting or hiring the head of any kind of reference department in all kinds of libraries in the United States. The two words have been frequently and interchangeably used in both business organizations and in academic institutions in such a way that they have become the household word when hiring people in all cadres of key positions in those organizations.

Leadership and management are subjects that have attracted considerable interest in the library field. Most researchers working in the area of leadership implicitly assume that leadership is a critical factor in the successful operation of any organization. A few have questioned this assumption and have suggested that other variables might help account for organizational effectiveness. These tend to be environmental influences such as market conditions, the industry, technology, governmental policies, and even factors like internal organizational politics (Gemmill and Oakley, 1992). The dominant principle of organization has shifted, from management in order to control an enterprise to leadership in order to bring out the best in people and to respond quickly to change (Naisbitt and Aburdene, 1990: 218). The library community and indeed our society are saturated with speakers, institutes, articles, books and events about the need for good management and better leadership (Sweeney, 1997: 32). In this era of high technological innovation in most types of libraries, the successful library leader must exercise creative leadership and management of the library's programs, services and resources.

Management and leadership are certainly not new topics but have greatly increased emphasis these days. This paper will attempt to focus on the issue of whether heads of reference departments in academic libraries of today are managers or leaders and at the same time attempt to address the traits, skills, and competencies those heads of reference should possess. In doing this, an effort will be made to define the terms "management" and "leadership," and later find out where the reference department head falls. It will examine the roles of the academic library department head and see how they can lead the reference department of the 21st century to its organizational effectiveness.

LITERATURE REVIEW

Management is the process of working with people and resources to accomplish organizational goals. Good managers do those things both effectively and efficiently. To be effective is to achieve organizational goals. To be efficient is to achieve goals with minimum waste of resources, that is, to make the best possible use of money, time, materials, and people. However, some managers fail on both criteria, or focus on one at the expense of another. The best managers maintain a clear focus on both effectiveness and efficiency. The management process when properly executed involves a wide variety of activities, including planning, organizing, leading, and controlling (Bateman and Snell, 1999: 6).

"Leadership is the ability to get work done with and through others while winning their respect, confidence, loyalty, and willing cooperation" (Plunkett, 1996: 359). "Leading is stimulating people to be high performers. It is directing, motivating, and communicating with people, helping guide and inspire them toward achieving team and organizational goals. Leading takes place in teams, departments, and at the top of organizations" (Bateman and Snell, 1999: 7). Intagliata et al. (2000) contend that leadership competencies are considered to be important in the achievement of organizational goals, particularly when the competencies are organization specific, for a number of reasons, including: (1) they guide direction, (2) they are measurable, (3) competencies can be learned, (4) they can distinguish and differentiate the organization, and (5) they can help integrate management practices.

Metz (2001) notes, today, effective library leadership requires an extraordinary ability to maintain a delicate and continually shifting balance in the management of technical, financial, and human resources to serve the academic mission of our colleges and universities.

Leaders must make judicious decisions that blend the strengths of the past, the demands of the present, and the uncertainty of the future, and they must do so continually–often within an organizational environment designed to support the past.

Clearly, "successful library leaders" will need to demonstrate "a blend of bold leadership, informed risk-taking, widespread consultation, and consensus building. They . . . will need keen analytical powers, abundant common sense, vibrant creativity, reasoned judgment, and a passionate commitment to the mission and goals of higher education." Metz concluded: "to develop this new leader is an enormous challenge" (p. 2-3).

LEADERSHIP AND MANAGEMENT PARADOX

McNamara (2002) states, traditionally (although many would now disagree), the term "management" is described as the functions of planning, organizing, leading and controlling (or coordinating) activities in an organization. "Managing" is explained as carrying out these activities. Courses in management often teach from this perspective. Some writers follow this view and believe that the activity of leading is but one aspect of management. Other writers disagree and assert that "managing" is planning, organizing, and controlling, and that "leading" is a distinctly separate activity that primarily involves influencing people. An old adage that follows from this latter view is "Leaders do the right things. Managers do things right." Another adage is "Leaders lead people, managers manage things." Other writers would even disagree with this view, however. They would assert that, although a person happens to be carrying out activities that influence others, if he or she does not hold a formal role in the organization with the title of manager then he or she is not a leader (pp. 2-4).

Riggs (1982) argues that management and leadership are two separate hemispheres. Managers tend to work within defined bounds of known quantities, using well-established techniques to accomplish predetermined ends; the manager tends to stress means and neglect ends. The leader's task is to hold, before all persons connected with an institution or organization, some vision of what its mission is and how it can be reached more effectively. Managers may be described as being too busy doing the possible to find time to reach for the difficult or impossible. Leadership involves looking forward, as well as inward (p. viii).

Leadership has its own problems. Bennis (1997) states that there is no simple solution to the leadership problem. But he does give us some insights of leadership of which we should be cognizant:

1. Leaders must develop the vision and strength to call the shots.
2. The leader must be a conceptualist. He or she must possess an entrepreneurial vision and a sense of perspective.
3. The leader must have a sense of continuity and significance.
4. The leader must get at the truth and learn how to filter the unwieldy flow of information into coherent patterns.
5. The leader must be a social architect who studies and shapes what is called the "culture of work."
6. The task of the leader is to lead. And to lead others s/he must first of all know him/herself and utilize his or her strengths to the benefit of the institution (pp. 45-46).

The Differences Between Management and Leadership

There are some obvious dichotomies when considering the two terms "management and leadership" as shown in the following chart by Kotter (1990).

The Differences Between Management and Leadership

Management	Leadership
Planning and Budgeting–establishing detailed steps and timetables for achieving needed results, and then allocating the resources necessary to make that happen	Establishing Direction–developing a vision of the future, often the distant future, and strategies for producing the changes needed to achieve that vision
Organizing and Staffing–establishing some structure for accomplishing plan requirements, staffing that structure with individuals, delegating responsibility and authority for carrying out the plan, providing policies and procedures to help guide people, and creating methods or systems to monitor implementation	Aligning People–communicating the direction by words and deeds to all those whose cooperation may be needed so as to influence the creation of teams and coalitions that understand the vision and strategies, and accept their validity
Controlling and Problem Solving–monitoring results versus plan in some detail, identifying deviations, and then planning and organizing to solve these problems	Motivating and Inspiring–energizing people to overcome major political, bureaucratic, and resource barriers to change by satisfying very basic, but often unfulfilled, human needs
Produces a degree of predictability and order, and has the potential of consistently producing key results expected by various stakeholders (for example, for customers, always being on time; for stockholders, being on budget)	Produces change, often to a dramatic degree, and has the potential of producing extremely useful change (for example, new products that customers want, new approaches to labor relations that help make a firm more competitive)

Source: *A Force for Change: How Leadership Differs from Management* by John P. Kotter (p. 6). Copyright © 1990 by John P. Kotter, Inc. Reprinted with the permission of The Free Press, a Division of Simon & Schuster. All rights reserved.

Management Hierarchy

Various managers stress different activities or exhibit different management styles and at different management levels. This happens also in libraries and at different levels of management. These individuals do not manage using identical techniques or styles. There are several reasons for these differences, including the managers' training, personalities, orientation and backgrounds. There are different kinds of managers who operate with different styles found at three different management levels in virtually all organizations: top-level, middle-level and lower-level.

Top-level managers are the senior executives of an organization and are responsible for the overall management and organizational effectiveness. In academic institutions, the equivalent of the top-level managers will be the president, provost or vice president for academic affairs and any other vice president within the institution.

Middle-level managers are found in the middle layers of the organizational hierarchy, reporting to top-level executives. In an academic library setting, the equivalent will be dean or director of libraries.

Front-line managers are lower-level managers that supervise the operational activities of the organization. Also in the academic library setting, the equivalent will be associate or assistant dean of libraries and department heads. Bateman and Snell (1999) explain that the front line managers or operational managers and department heads are directly involved with non-management employees, implementing the specific plans developed with middle managers. This role is critical in the organization, because operational managers are the link between management and non-management personnel (pp. 10-12). Let us take a few minutes to reflect on the leadership traits and skills of an effective leader in an organization.

Leadership Traits and Skills

The list below demonstrates the leadership traits and skills that are very necessary for an effective leader. This set of traits and skills may be recommended for the reference department head in any kind of library setting:

Traits and Skills Commonly Associated with Leader Effectiveness

Traits	Skills
Adaptable to situation	Clever (intelligent)
Alert to social environment	Conceptually skilled
Ambitious and achievement oriented	Creative
Assertive	Diplomatic and tactful
Cooperative	Fluent in speaking
Decisive	Knowledgeable about group task
Dependable	Organized (administrative ability)
Dominant (desire to influence others)	Persuasive
Energetic (high activity level)	Socially skilled
Persistent	
Self-confident	
Tolerant of stress	
Willing to assume responsibility	

Source: *Leadership in Organizations* by Yukl, Gary A. © Reprinted by permission of Pearson Education, Inc., Upper Saddle River, NJ.

ROLES OF THE REFERENCE DEPARTMENT HEAD
IN THE NEW MILLENNIUM

The reference department head plays a very key role in the day-to-day running of the department. This individual should be a transformational leader. The department reference head keeps lines of communication open and provides one-on-one monitoring to develop his or her employees. The department head should have a vision for the department. Riggs (1984) asserts:

> In a library setting, the department head plays a central role in the strategic planning process. Along with professional members of the director's office, the department heads constitute the majority of the members of the planning team. A few selected/elected representatives below the department head-level may assist the director with strategic planning. Since strategic planning is essentially a "top-down" process, the department head holds a key position in shaping the future of the library. Many of the goals, objectives, and strategies will most likely be realized through the activities of the departments. Since departments generally have a symbiotic relationship with one another, close cooperation and open communication are required.
>
> Department heads are indispensable in the introduction and implementation of strategic planning. Nevertheless, in many instances, they have to undergo an attitude change about the planning process. They must be able to perceive how change resulting from proper planning can facilitate constructive interrelationships among the various departments. (pp. 15-16)

Reference department heads in academic libraries do all kinds of things from reference desk duties to even keeping library security after Sept. 11, 2001. Sometimes one will be tempted to call reference librarians and their department heads "Jack of all trades and master of none." Some other responsibilities of the reference department head, skills, and traits are summarized below.

Responsibilities

- Coordinating
- Staff training

- Research
- Supervision
- Administrative
- Scheduling
- Staff hiring
- Partnership building
- Reference Collection Development
- Information Literacy and Library Instruction
- Information Technology
- Planning

Skills Needed for a Reference Department Head

- Effective Communication: Oral and Written
- Interpersonal
- Flexible and Adaptable
- Negotiation
- Organizational
- Time Management

Traits That a Reference Department Head Should Have

- Courageous
- Decisive
- Dependable
- Judgment
- Sensibility
- Loyalty
- Enthusiasm
- Endurance
- Initiative

Other qualifications required of a new library leader that will be applicable to a reference department head are listed by Pritchard and Marquardt (2000). They contend that the standard set of qualifications listed in vacancy notices includes skills in management, leadership, planning, budget, communication, collaborative decision making, staff development, fund raising, knowledge of trends in technology and higher education, and, of course, "vision" (p. 2).

COMPETENCIES REQUIRED
OF REFERENCE DEPARTMENT HEADS

The following recent job advertisements posted in *American Libraries* (Hot Jobs Online) demonstrate some competencies, skills, qualifications, and roles required of new department heads of reference:

HEAD OF REFERENCE

XYZ University seeks qualified candidates for the following position: **HEAD OF REFERENCE** Under the direction of the Director of Research and Information Access Services, the successful candidate will be expected to provide the leadership necessary to develop comprehensive, first class reference services to the university community. Specifically, the successful candidate will supervise the reference desk, including scheduling, monitoring and evaluating service quality, evaluating employee performance and providing reference desk coverage, develop goals and objectives for the reference department, envision and implement innovative projects and services in response to the needs of the university community, identify and evaluate emerging information technologies for implementation, formulate and recommend departmental policies, coordinate documentation of procedures and services, prepare and submit reports to administration as requested, develop initiatives for outreach of reference services to faculty, coordinate Reference Collection Management in collaboration with assigned liaisons, coordinate graduate research liaison, develop and coordinate management of specific in-house resources, teach classes in Information Literacy program as needed in cooperation with Head of Information Literacy, general collection management responsibilities as assigned and in cooperation with the Director of Collection Management. Some weekend and evening hours are required. (American Libraries (Hot Jobs Online))

SHOULD THE HEAD OF REFERENCE
BE HIRED FROM OUTSIDE THE PROFESSION?

The head of reference services for the 21st century should be an experienced librarian who will be in a position to win the trust of his or her fellow librarians and staff members. This individual should be a librarian who possesses the good leadership skills, traits, and qualities in dealing with the public and all employees. Some libraries have hired people who have some managerial experience, but no library experience, to be head of their reference departments. The danger with that type of practice is that it does not build trust within employees in the department.

Hiring from outside the field will not give proper credence and legitimacy to the profession and it will bring a lot of mixed feelings and bad blood among the reference department staff. Other reasons why it is not advisable to hire department head of reference services from managers who are not librarians are:

- Librarianship is a profession and like other professions, there should be a set of rules and regulations governing and guiding it.
- Minimum educational qualification of an American Library Association (ALA) accredited Master's degree in Library or Information Science is required and must be met.
- Some years of professional experience in the library and information science arena will be needed.
- Good and effective communication skills will be absolutely necessary:
  - Knowledge of the library, nuances, lingoes, isms, and jargons associated with the profession and frequently used when interpreting the deluge of resources and technology at the reference desk.

Judging from the above reasons, it will be prudent to consider a librarian with experience, and especially in reference services, the first opportunity to be head of reference before considering a manager who has no library experience or is a non-librarian. A manager without library experience will have a great disadvantage. A librarian who has read the drug literature and has studied drug interaction with the body cannot claim to be a doctor or a pharmacist without adequate training and licenses. The same argument will be appropriate for us to say that an experienced manager, say, from a grocery store, may not be an effective library leader or a good head of academic library reference.

However, with adequate and proper training in reference service, there is still a place for an experienced librarian to head a reference department. This should require some cross-training of that librarian to acquire some skills and competencies required of a reference department head. Sometimes, this potential and aspiring new reference department head should be filling in at the reference desk for a period of time and learning the patron needs, their patterns of questions and day-to-day operational needs of the reference department.

Another point in favor of hiring experienced librarians from other parts of the library is that their experience counts, and they may also have been reference librarians at some point during their career path. Their training will take less of library financial and personnel resources. So, this idea will be less expensive to the library.

Finally, considering the current declining economic climate and budget woes facing today's academic libraries, it will be cost-effective and reasonable to fill vacant reference department head positions from a pool of experienced librarians already employed at those libraries. This concept will be better than hiring a non-professional librarian manager who has no knowledge of libraries to run an academic library reference department. Hiring a reference department head from outside of the library profession will ultimately demean the profession and cause a perpetual professional rift.

CONCLUSION

Reference librarianship has experienced tremendous change in the last decade. One of the causes of this rapid change is due to the infusion of technology in the operation of reference services. Technology has seriously affected the way reference librarians and their leaders perform their duties. New methods and approaches have to be introduced for reference librarians to be capable of handling the mixed array of questions coming at the reference desk. It requires reference librarians who have the skills, training and experience to comfort and assist the patrons at the new millennium reference desk.

It takes a good and effective head of reference to lead the troops and to steer the department wheel in the right direction. Every library deserves a good leader. All reference departments deserve good department heads that will be approachable, creative, tenacious, dependable and honest. They must do good service for their departments and follow through on ideas and assignments. The reference department head must possess some time management skills and must be able to prioritize routinely to meet the deluge of demands at the reference desk. The department head of reference services should be both a leader and manager.

Finally, while commenting on commitment to service, Sherrer (1998) states: "Good service, however, is the result of personal commitment and idealism tempered with reasonableness that combines to produce satisfied users. Paradigms aside, libraries are only as good as their front lines. Their consistency, success, and value are judged at that point. In today's world, that front line may be a person or a computer screen but in either case it must be friendly, approachable, intuitive, and service centered. All of these attributes however must be driven by a commitment to service the public" (p. 16).

REFERENCES

American Libraries, (Hot Jobs Online). Feb. 4, 2003.

Bateman, Thomas S. and Scott A. Snell. (1999). *Management: Building a Competitive Advantage*, 4th ed., Boston: Irwin/McGraw-Hill.

Bennis, Warren G. (1977). "Where Have All the Headers Gone?" *Technology Review*, 79 (March/April): 45-46.

Gemmill, Gary and Judith, Oakley. (1992). "Leadership: An Alienating Social Myth?" *Human Relations*, 45 (Feb.): 113-29.

Hersberger, Rodney. (1997). "Leadership and Management of Technological Innovation in Academic Libraries." *Library Administration & Management*, 11 (1): 26-29.

Intagliata, Jim, Dave Ulrich and Norm Smallwood. (2002). "Levering Leadership Competencies to Produce Leadership Brand: Creating Distinctiveness by Focusing on Strategy and Results." *Human Resource Planning*. 23. Available online http:// proquest.umi.com/pdqweb.

Kotter, John P. (1990). *A Force for Change: How Leadership Differs from Management*, N.Y.: The Free Press, 6.

Mech, Terrence F. (1993). "The Managerial Decision Styles of Academic Library Directors." *College & Research Libraries* (Sept): 375-386.

Metz, Terry. (2001). "Wanted: Library Leaders for a Discontinuous Future," *Library Issues* (Jan) 21: no. 3, 2-3.

McNamara, Carter. (2002) "Guidelines to Understand Literature About Leadership" (pp. 1-4): available online from http://www.mapnp.org/library/ldrship/ldng_lit.htm.

Moore, Audrey D. "Reference Librarianship: It Was the Best of Times, It Was . . . " *The Reference Librarian*, 54: 3-10.

Naisbitt, John and Patricia Aburdene. (1990). *Megatrends 2000: The New Directions for the 1990's*. NY: Morrow, 218.

Plunkett, W. Richard. (1996). *Supervision: Diversity and Teams in the Workplace*. 8th ed. New Jersey: Prentice-Hall.

Pritchard, Sarah M. and Steven Marquardt, (2000). "Looking for Director Goodboss: How to Recruit a Head Librarian." *Library Issues*, 21 (Sept.): 2.

Riggs, Donald E. (ed.) (1982). *Library Leadership: Visualizing the Future*. Phoenix, Arizona: The Oryx Press.

Riggs, Donald E. (1984), *Strategic Planning for Library Managers*, Phoenix, Arizona: The Oryx Press.

Sherrer, Johannah. (1996). "Thriving in Changing Times: Competencies for Today's Reference Librarians" *The Reference Librarian*, 54: 11-20.

Sweeney, Richard. (1997). "Leadership Skills in the Reengineered Library" *Library Administration & Management*, 11 (1): 30-41.

Yukl, Gary A. (1981). *Leadership in Organizations*, Englewood Cliffs, NJ: Prentice Hall: 70.

Index

failure to provide, 56-57
in formal routines, 52
in informal routines, 52-53
need for, 52-53
open training milieu of, 53,55,57
self-disclosure in, 55,57
supervisory working alliance
    development in, 55-56,57
as technique, 54
traits of, 112
    desired, 23-24
H-E-A-R-T management approach, 41
Hierarchical management model, 75,77,
    78,109-110
Hiring
of heads of reference
    advertisements used in, 94
    guidelines for, 113-115
of staffing, 6-7,9,48-49

Indiana University-Purdue University,
    University Libraries, 77
Internet, heads of reference familiarity
    with, 20

Jennings' Variables in Library Cultural
    Diversity, 28
Job applicants, assessment of, 6-7

King, Geraldine, 77

Leaders
    responsibilities of, 108
    traits and skills of, 110
Leadership
    collaborative, 65-67
    definition of, 37,38,61,107
    differentiated from management, 37,
        108-109
    employee-centered, 37,44
    leader-follower relationship in, 60,
        61-62

relationship with organizational
    effectiveness, 106
role in organizational change, 61-62
styles of, 38
task-centered, 37,44
training for, 67
transactional, 61
transforming, 61,64-65
Leadership (Burns), 60-61
"Leadership in the Post-Hierarchical
    Library" (Sweeney), 63
Leadership in the Twenty First Century
    (Rost), 3,61-62
Leading, definition of, 37,108
Lewis, David, 77
LIBQUAL, 27
Librarians. *See also* Academic librarians;
    Public librarians; Reference
    librarians; Substitute librarians
    shortage of, 52
Library administration, job openings in,
    18
Library directors, as reference
    department supervisors, 22
Library instruction, 92-93,98-99,101-102
    for faculty, 101
    need for, 101
    in use of electronic resources, 62,74,
        101-102
*Library Issues Briefing for Faculty and
    Administrators,* 66
"Library Leaders for the 21st Century"
    (Martin), 66

Management, 75-86
    collective, 75,76
    collegial, 24-26,78,82
    components of, 72-73,107
    continuing education in, 25-26
    definition of, 75,106-108
    differentiated from leadership, 37,
        108-109
    H-E-A-R-T approach in, 41
    hierarchical, 75,77,78,109-110

Ethics and Reference Services, edited by Bill Katz and Ruth A. Fraley, MLS, MBA (No. 4, 1982). *Library experts discuss the major ethical and legal implications that reference librarians must take into consideration when handling sensitive inquiries about confidential material.*

Reference Services Administration and Management, edited by Bill Katz and Ruth A. Fraley, MLS, MBA (No. 3, 1982). *Librarianship experts discuss the management of the reference function in libraries and information centers, outlining the responsibilities and qualifications of reference heads.*

Reference Services in the 1980s, edited by Bill Katz (No. 1/2, 1982). *Here is a thought-provoking volume on the future of reference services in libraries, with an emphasis on the challenges and needs that have come about as a result of automation.*